CHURCH STAFF EVALUATION

A Tool For Effective Performance

Compiled And Edited By Joyce Parchman, Director Of Publications

NACBA PRESS

Church Staff Evaluation
A Tool for Effective Performance

Compiled and edited by Joyce Parchman, Director of Publications

Projects completed as a part of the NACBA Certification process:

Performance Evaluation by Simeon May, FCBA

Job Descriptions For A Church Staff by B.C. Guffey, FCBA

A Performance Appraisal Strategy by James L. Murphy, FCBA

Developing A Performance/Team Contribution Evaluation Procedure by Edward R. Lycett, FCBA

The Development Of Job Descriptions And Performance Evaluations by Louise C. Gee, FCBA

Introducing A Personnel Manual To A Smaller Congregation by Dr. W. Maynard Pittendreigh, Jr., FCBA

NACBA Ledger articles and other sources

Authors

Simeon May, FCBA, is Executive Director of the National Association of Church Business Administration.

B.C. Guffey, FCBA, is Administrator at Quail Springs Baptist Church, Oklahoma City, Oklahoma.

James L. Murphy, FCBA, is Director of Ministries and Administrator at Saint Paul United Methodist Church, Louisville, Kentucky.

Edward Lycett, FCBA, is Pastor of Education/ Administration at Shirley Hills Baptist Church, Warner Robins, Georgia.

Louise Gee, FCBA, is a retired administrator who served at St. Luke's United Methodist Church, Midland, Texas.

Maynard Pittendreigh, Jr., FCBA, is Pastor of Sonrise Presbyterian Church, Miami, Florida.

ISBN: 0-9705433-1-X

©1999, 2001 by National Association of Church Business Administration

NACBA Press is the publishing arm of the National Association of Church Business Administration.

NACBA
PRESS

100 N. Central Expy. • Suite 914
Richardson, Texas 75080-5326
(800) 898-8085 • (972) 699-7555
(972) 699-7617 Fax
www.nacba.net

TABLE OF CONTENTS

Chapter One

THE CHURCH STAFF

B.C. Guffey, FCBA

Introduction

A church is engaged in the most important business on earth—proclaiming the gospel to every person. The church staff is an important, critical, vital church resource.

Churches also have business affairs because they are engaged in an enterprise that receives and disburses monies, employs persons, keeps records, provides food services, has legal obligations and owns property. To handle these affairs in the most effective way, is a matter of Christian stewardship. God has given each church a mission to achieve and the resources to achieve that mission. A church has a moral and spiritual duty to manage its resources effectively.[1]

A successful, growing church of the future means more than increased attendance, more buildings, and larger budgets. It means developing the people power available in the church, and mobilizing the members for achieving the church's mission. Here, church management comes into focus as a means of pulling together all resources (including staff members), and deciding on the best ways to achieve the church's objective.

Pastors and leaders alike must realize that good management principles will enhance their ministry. Proper administration will move a church along a definite path to reaching its goals and objectives.[2] One part of proper administration for a church staff is well-written, usable, up-to-date job descriptions.

The Church Staff

Does a church need a staff? There comes a time when one person cannot do it all. Although volunteer assistance and committees are invaluable in providing leadership to get things done in the church, at some point people with training and expertise are needed to direct and take responsibility for the daily operations of the church. In time,

each area of ministry may develop a need for support personnel.

Whether a church staff consists of two or two dozen, the focus should be on only one mission: furthering the gospel of Jesus Christ through the work of the local congregation.[3]

It has been correctly stated that a church will not exceed the quality of its leadership. No segment of leadership effectiveness is more crucial than the church's employed leaders.

Although some staff groups have interpersonal problems, many staffs function poorly because of ineffective recruiting, orientation, administration, and performance evaluation.[4] The number of paid staffs in churches may vary, but their purpose is to perform tasks that support and sustain the five common functions of a church: to preach the gospel; to worship; to educate the members; to perform church ministries; and to apply the teachings to life. The church's mission is the staff's mission. The church's goals are the staff's goals.

This concept places a grave responsibility on the pastor and other supervisors to lead staff workers to reach and maintain high levels of workmanship and interpersonal relationships.[5]

There is nothing more important in any company than its human resources. These resources must be effectively managed if the company and its people are to prosper and grow. This is not a new principle, but in many churches its implications are often forgotten or ignored.

What is more difficult than the problem of dealing with people and minimizing interpersonal friction? What is more time consuming, and what results are more impossible to measure accurately? It is easy to rationalize and accept the fact that many managers are inclined to devote their energies, time and attention to the more practical problems of production, not people; marketing, not men; computers, not co-workers. This is one of the more difficult and serious aspects of the manager's job.[6]

The modern office manager spends the great majority of the day working with people, inspiring them to use their highest abilities and skills, striving to develop them, and helping them to achieve satisfaction and the fulfillment of their personal needs through their work efforts and accomplishments. Why these extraordinary personnel efforts? Basically for two reasons. First, people are the most important resource that the office manager utilizes. Office activities are of, by, and for people. Second, people are not like any other resource. They behave in widely different and complicated ways and their behaviors are neither consistent nor readily predictable.[7]

Most pastors and other staff supervisors want to be a part of a well-managed staff. So do the secretaries, receptionists, clerks and custodians.

Building and maintaining a well-managed staff begins by getting the right person for each job. The quality, dedication and morale of the paid staff contribute greatly to the overall attainment of a church's goals.

Quality shows in a number of ways, including evidence of spiritual concern and a genuine desire to serve. Letters neatly typed and framed on the page speak well of a church. Attractive church bulletins create favorable positive attitudes toward the church's total program. Accurate office and educational records provide incentives to volunteer workers who have Sunday record-keeping duties. The receptionist creates goodwill for the church when she receives visitors, members and vendors cordially and helpfully.[8]

A church becomes aware of the need for job descriptions when it desires to improve efficiency and alleviate conflicts and misunderstandings in the decision-making process.

Structure and organization are important in the local church and should be given much attention. Many people problems are really organizational problems, and originate from inadequate organizational patterns or from insufficient policies or operational guidelines.

The personality and ability of each staff member must be respected, and job descriptions should be written with enough flexibility to allow for these individual differences. The job description should enable the staff member to operate more effectively and efficiently, and care must be taken to avoid a negative, restrictive and legalistic philosophy.[9]

A negative approach is easily obtained when thinking in terms of procedures, rules, regulations, job descriptions and policies. These can convey the idea of keeping something from happening through the staff and the church instead of enabling something to happen. A staff may be so bound by rigid job descriptions that there is little chance for free expression of creative thinking and acting or expressing real differences of opinions. Yet, so much informality and laxity in methods and procedures may prevail that once again individual differences may be hidden or unexpressed. The need is for the use of procedures, techniques and job descriptions which might aid and affect decision making.[10]

A necessary step toward an enabling philosophy in the preparation of staff job descriptions is a commitment to simplicity. People tend to equate words, systems and procedures with red tape and needless complexity, but in the church, when the procedures and job descriptions are simplified and basic, the better they are for effectiveness, efficiency and morale.[11]

People are of supreme importance in the local church; since they are different and their needs are different, job descriptions should always be written in a flexible manner to better meet these needs. Flexibility helps undergird the enabling philosophy. The feeling conveyed by the enabling philosophy will build within the staff the desire to accomplish God's will and purpose for the church, and will draw them together in a positive commitment to each other and to the church.[12]

All in all, paid staff can affect the general attitude and optimism of the entire church. The church, then, has a vital interest in the quality and dedication of its staff workers. The pastor and other staff supervisors, with the help of the personnel committee, have the responsibility of obtaining the best possible workers.[13]

Performance appraisal is an important aspect of the effective utilization of human resources.

Notes

[1] Marvin Myers, *Managing The Business Affairs Of The Church*, Convention Press, Nashville, 1981, Foreward

[2] Ibid., p. 5

[3] Ibid., p. 13

[4] Leonard E. Wedel, *Building And Maintaining A Church Staff*, Broadman, Nashville, 1966, Foreward

[5] Ibid., p. 10

[6] Elizabeth Marting, Ed, *AMA Book of Employment Forms*, AMA, 1976, p. 17

[7] Terry and Stallard, *Office Mangement And Control*, Richard D. Irwin, 1980, p. 399

[8] Wedel, p. 10

[9] Robert A. Young, *The Development of a Church Manual of Administrative Policies*, Bel-Air Church Directory Publishers, Inc., 1975, p. IV

[10] Ibid., p. 10

[11] Julian Feldman, *Church Purchasing Procedures*, Englewood Cliffs, NJ, Prentice Hall, Inc. 1964, p. 42

[12] Young, p. 14

[13] Wedel, p. 10

Chapter Two
PERSONNEL EVALUATION

Personnel evaluation, rating, classification, appraisal, analysis, development review, or contribution analysis—regardless of what you call it, most managers and supervisors fear it. It is an awesome thing to be responsible for the task of evaluating another human being.

Most staff members want to know how they are doing. Although there are those who will follow blindly, the most effective followers are those who have a clear picture of what they are expected to do. Their first question is, "Am I doing what I agreed to do?" The second question is, "If I am not, what needs to be done by me, the organization or my leaders to permit me to be successful?"

An appraisal system that seeks to move the employee to more maturity will increase the personal satisfaction of the employee and gain productivity for the employer.

Test It Out

Too often there is a wide divergence of understanding between the supervisor and the supervised as to what is expected. A good test of this is to write down a list of five to ten key things, which you expect each of your subordinates to do. (If possible, keep it to five.) Then ask the subordinate to make a similar list of the key things that he or she believes that you expect of them. If you have a 90 percent agreement, you are doing well.

But suppose you discover, as is often the case, wide areas of disagreement. What should you do? The answer is an effective personnel evaluation system.

An evaluation that focuses on an agreed set of objectives places the questions of personality, relationships, personal problems, and other areas in proper perspective.[1]

Definition

A performance review can be defined as a team meeting scheduled to review commonly agreed upon goals; discuss the employee's contribution; explore necessary work performance adjustments; agree upon short- and long-range goals, actions and support; and to communicate salary decisions.[2]

A performance appraisal or employee review is an organized, systematic approach to evaluate an employee's job performance.[3]

To appraise is to put a value on something. To place a value on anything, one must have criteria or standards by which the value is to be determined.

The Basis For Employee Appraisals[4]

Examples

Sally was called by the pastor and asked to resign. She was surprised. She had no idea that she was about to lose her job. She had received some suggestions in the past on how to improve her work. She had communicated with the volunteer with whom she was having problems and thought things were okay. Before that, she had met with her supervisor and was told there were problems, and plans were made to change. However, there was no formal appraisal, no communication with the pastor, and no indication of the consequences of a failure to respond to the suggestions.

Because there had not been good communication, the request to resign was rescinded by the staff parish committee, and Sally was asked to change responsibilities so she would not be working with the volunteer in the area which was causing her problems. The change took her out of immediate risk of losing her job. But two things happened. Another employee was asked to perform tasks for which Sally was hired, and Sally was asked to work in areas which were not her specialty and for which she was not as prepared. The result was that finally she quit.

John was not getting his work done. As a part-time custodian, he was responsible for cleaning the new education and office wing of the church building. He was scheduled for twenty hours a week. Because the church wanted someone in the building during the evenings for security reasons, John was hired to work from 5:00 p.m. to 9:00 p.m. each weeknight.

John had another job during the day, which made it hard for him to come to work at 5:00 p.m. Several changes were made in his church schedule to accommodate his other work and home obligations. Eventually he was working just a couple of hours each night and making up the remainder of the twenty hours on Saturday. This caused several problems. There was never a set time, he was not getting all the work done, and there were indications that he was reporting time worked overnight or on Saturday when there were questions about his being on the job.

A meeting was set up in which very specific work hours were defined, specific tasks for each work period were set out, and a warning was issued that failure to comply would result in his dismissal.

His response was to conform to the requirements and do his work. He also began taking more interest in the appearance of the part of the building for which he was responsible, suggesting ways to do more than was required.

Christian Basis For Employee Performance Appraisal

One of the first areas to explore regarding appraisals is taking a Christian approach to dealing with persons, especially those employed by the church. There are standards by which we should deal with employees—the standards demonstrated by Jesus.

James F. Hind illustrated the possibility of reaping corporate benefits by applying Christian principles. In one of his stories, he relates how Wayne Alderson turned around a failing steel foundry. Alderson

accomplished this by developing a "Value of the Person" concept and applying it to all his employees. He identified the three key ingredients that made this concept succeed as "*love, dignity, and respect.* He understood that worker morale and reconciliation come from the way people are treated."[5]

"Anderson's story is living proof that God's ways can succeed in the workplace, even in the worst of business situations. His 'Value of the Person' program strikes at the very heart of the approach proposed in this book: *The belief that all people have inherent value by virtue of being created in the image of God, and thus inherent right to develop to their fullest potential.*"[6]

Jesus Christ: The Manager

Jesus gave us the second greatest command—to love others as ourselves. He told us and demonstrated to us that "in the kingdom of God, service to others is the true measurement of greatness." Jesus didn't use the hard sell to get things done. "Rather, He wooed and courted His listeners, never forgetting their needs."

"Jesus Christ understood that self-motivation is to be cherished and nurtured among others, and He did just that."

"If there was one modern management trait that carried Jesus Christ from a nobody to a somebody, it was His service to and for the benefit of others— His *servant leadership.*"[7]

Judge With Your Heart First

Part of Hind's approach is expressed in his "servant leadership" style.

Managers should view themselves as *developers of people*, not as *"take charge" heroes.*

Servant leadership does not abolish the necessary demands a good manager must place upon others, such as competency, obedience, discipline, excellence, and hard work. It does bring an added dimension to effective management. Servant leadership gets close to the heart of the matter. It combines a servant heart—soft, feeling, generous with a corporate mind—tough-minded, realistic thought.

Feelings are the most powerful human motivators, not pay raises, not a title on the door and a carpet on the floor, not a corner office, not fabulous fringe benefits—but feelings.

"The first commandment (of caring) says that in developing and motivating others to succeed, you must lead with sincere feelings, setting your own importance aside and saying, "I want to see people succeed. I am going to help people develop." This shows people that you care about them. Ultimately, this is what enlists their devotion. This is Christian love in practice, and it pulls (not pushes) people to do bigger and better things."[8]

Using Spiritual Gifts[9]

The New Testament abounds with the mention of spiritual gifts (1 Corinthians 12; Romans 12; Ephesians 4). In 1 Peter, we are told, *"Each person has received a special gift, employ it in serving one another."*

1st Corinthians 12:27–28, in speaking of spiritual gifts, says, " . . .you are the body of Christ and each one of you is a part of it." In verse 26: "If one part suffers, every part suffers with it, if one part is honored every part rejoices with it."

"We are to grow up in . . . Him . . . from whom the whole body, being fitted and held together by that which every joint supplies, according to the proper working of each individual part, causing the growth of the body for the building up of itself in love." (Ephesians 4:15-16) This is both 1) missional in the world and 2) edifying in the body.

In all of the above scriptural quotations the underlying theological assumptions speak to the nature of God, humankind and the church. God is the giver of each gift, and God bestows on each varieties of gifts. The gifts from God are to be used to build up the church to serve others in the world. According to 1st Corinthians, no gift is more important than another, and each person is urged to employ that gift to the best of his/her ability. When any fail to use the gift, all suffer.

Since St. Paul uses the analogy that the church is like a physical body, it is therefore assumed that all (employed staff and laity) have their proper place and function within the body of Christ. What St.

Paul does not address directly and what the church wrestles with is the question about 1) poor performance/growth and development, 2) failure to assume responsibility/asserting too much responsibility and 3) termination of employment/search and hiring. Job descriptions, self evaluations and performance evaluations use tools to define expectations and tasks so that each person may maximize his/her gifts and develop his/her potential.

Christ promises grace and redemption. The tougher task may be the rehabilitation of a staff employee (or volunteer) through counseling and job evaluation rather than termination.

Human beings tend to rise to the level of their defined expectations. Job descriptions and evaluations can be instruments to affirm persons, not primarily to get them to be greater and more efficient producers. They are God's creation and worthy of praise, correction, restoration and help.

People have various strengths, gifts and competencies and can accomplish certain tasks with an extraordinary degree of achievement. The art is . . . to match those competencies with tasks related to a key objective so that people can put their gifts and competencies to work in ways that count.

Treat Employees Fairly[10]

Remember then, you employers, that your responsibility is to be fair and just toward those whom you employ, never forgetting that you yourselves have a heavenly employer.
Colossians 4:1, Phillips

Church employees need to be treated fairly in regard to employee development. This includes praise as well as constructive criticism. If we are going to take the time to search for the proper person to fill a position and spend time and money in training a person, we should be willing to help this person grow in his/her work by setting goals and standards and then correcting his/her course toward achieving those goals.

Establishing a performance evaluation system is no easy task, but it should be done in all churches for every level of staff.

Strive For Excellence[11]

Dealing with the subject of "developing performance reviews," whether in the secular world or in church work, is like opening a large can of worms. In my research, I found that "performance reviews" are sometimes viewed with disdain out in the real world as well as in the church.

Too many times today, individuals have an idea that just because they work for the church, the standards are different or nonexistent. In a survey distributed for this project, a pastor commented:

> *I believe pastors, staff, as well as all Christians, are under God's grace. If we pursue a heavy evaluation process like the world does, then we require them to live under the law. This is neither biblical nor practical where kingdom work is at hand. There must be a strong element of Trust among the staff. This is impossible to establish where there is the bondage of law. Worldly methods of evaluation create that bondage.*
>
> *Why do we continue to think that God's business, "Kingdom business," must be run in the same manner as the world?*
>
> *I wish you well with your project. However, I believe it to be a philosophy of the world, not of God.*
>
> *Sorry, but you asked.*

Unfortunately, this is not an uncommon notion in any type of workplace. There is a part of me that understands this position. There are times when I let my guard down, not wanting to be evaluated. That is probably when I am not doing my best. Then I remember that I was called to be a disciple, which means that I pattern my life after Jesus Christ, and nowhere in the scripture can I find where He had a bad day. My feelings are the same as George Sweeting when he said,

> "Long ago I made the decision to put my faith in the Lord Jesus Christ rather than in the visible things of this world. Have you welcomed Jesus Christ into your life so that He can live His life in you? Once you do, you have begun to walk the path to excellence. Excellence begins with a decision to receive Jesus as Savior and Lord."

For any Christian in any profession, excellence ought to be the norm and not the exception. For anyone working on a church staff, it should not even be questioned.

> "The desire for excellence, contrary to the thinking of some, is not crass or carnal but rather a divine, implanted desire to mimic God—to do as He does— . . .God calls us to climb higher. Excellence, by definition, means 'the very finest.' Just as one quality person motivates others to strive for excellence, so mediocrity spreads like a plague."[13]
>
> "The dictionary defines mediocrity as 'ordinary, neither good nor bad, barely adequate, poor, inferior.' Mediocrity is like playing five strings on a ten-stringed instrument. It is typing with five fingers and one eye rather than ten fingers and two eyes. It is a person with eagle talent thrashing his wings like a prairie chicken and flying no more than three feet off the ground. It is the individual with jet power doing push cart work. Mediocrity is crawling on hands and knees when we were created to stand, walk, run, and even mount up like an eagle and fly. Dare I say that scores of workers are mediocre? Many clerical workers don't earn their salaries, and hundreds of clergymen and teachers are painfully boring and dull."[14]

Through our calling in church administration, we deal with different individuals that God has led us to work with in the church office environment as well as in the congregation. Because of this, we should approach our responsibilities with excellence and a higher view of what we do.

A church office environment should not be an accident, but should be a well-executed plan of personal as well as physical "tools" with which to accomplish the tasks. The staff leader then takes on a lot of responsibility in developing the staff team as well as the development of a "theology of excellence." Just as a bad apple can spoil the whole barrel, so can a bad attitude change the atmosphere and the overall work production of the office. It can also spread to the church as a whole. So as we lead and develop our leadership role, we should develop a definition of management which is defined as well as practiced as . . . *"meeting the needs of people as they work at accomplishing their jobs."*[15]

This gives us the opportunities to develop the skills of equippers in accomplishing the biblical mandate of Ephesians 4:

> *I therefore, the prisoner of the Lord, entreat you to walk in a manner worthy of the calling with which you have been called, with all humility and gentleness, with patience, showing forbearance to one another in love... for the equipping of the saints for the work of service to the building up of the body of Christ; until we all attain to the unity of the faith, and of the knowledge of the Son of God to a mature man to the measure of the stature which belongs to the fullness of Christ.*
>
> Ephesians 4:1–2; 12–13

As we work with those whom we serve, we approach our work under different levels of performance and excellence. Because of this, members of our congregations develop perceptions about us and expect the same, or even a higher level of dedication, as we "perform" in our jobs as they have in theirs. However, we also have to deal with the difference between what they do and what we do. This has led Myron Rush to say, "Christians are discovering that the secular philosophy of management and leadership often conflicts with the Christian values. Many Christian leaders are looking for an alternative approach to management."

For us as disciples of Jesus Christ, that can only come from and through His word.

Successful Organization

The story of "The Tower of Babel" found in Genesis 11 is not an example of individuals following "the Lord thy God with all their heart," but it does give some very strong key ingredients of a successful organization.

Commitment to work on a goal

The people of Babel accepted a challenge. They chose to work toward a common end. A successful church is one whose church staff is working toward a common goal or vision for the church. This needs to be a shared vision where each staff member, no matter what the task or responsibility, takes part in bringing that to pass.

Unity among the people

They not only had a commitment to the task, they had a unity that was unparalleled. They had an understanding of what they wanted to do and how to do it. Their purpose became the most important thing in the world to them, yet they were up to no good. As we accomplish our tasks, we are at the greatest business in the world.

An effective communication system

Because of their common commitment and unity, they knew from where each other was coming. They experienced a common language. Just because individuals speak the same language does not necessarily mean they hear each other. When there is a commonality of spirit, there is an understanding of direction.

Doing the will of God

Even though this is a negative example of a "people" finding the will of God, when people have a commonality of vision, spirit and communication, they are on the way toward knowing what God would have them be and do. As they seek to accomplish what God has given them to do, they are in the center, seeking His will. And that is our calling . . . our task!

To sum it up, as we are developing a theology of excellence and incorporating this "theology" into our work,

> A philosophy of measuring performance must be based on the concept that the process is worthwhile and will be beneficial both to the church and to the staff member. The purpose should always be related to the goal of improving the performance of personnel so that the mission of the church can be accomplished... legal ramifications aside, to approach the subject in a haphazard manner is poor management, poor stewardship, and less than Christian. A proper approach will include carefully analyzed steps in determining the effectiveness of all personnel. Persons who

work for the church are accountable to God as well as to the church for their work. Paul's admonition in 1 Corinthians 4:2 is appropriate at this point: "It is required of stewards that one be found trustworthy."[17]

Evaluation: An Important Tool[18]

"It takes so much to have a good evaluation system that most of us don't even get started. No one wants to be a 'bad guy,' particularly a religious worker. Evaluation is not a bad thing; it's just perceived as that because of poor implementation." Those words came from a frustrated church business administrator (CBA) who responded to my survey. Many pastors and CBAs expressed similar feelings. Performance evaluations are generally viewed unfavorably, and many supervisors perceive them as time-wasters with little meaning or value.[19]

On the other hand, Myron Rush explains that "of all the tools at the manager's disposal, the performance evaluation is one of the most important and valuable. When properly designed and executed, it becomes the vehicle through which the organization's philosophy of management is communicated, trust is established, decision-making power is transferred, mistakes are turned into positive learning experiences, proper recognition is given, and both subordinate's and supervisor's productivity are increased."[20]

The lack of a performance evaluation system can certainly cause problems. A poorly performing employee who is not given instruction and correction will have expectations of a raise or a promotion. Then, should his work continue to deteriorate, the supervisor may be forced to terminate an employee who either has no idea his work is unsatisfactory or has been given a good performance review.[21]

While only 48 percent of the survey participants indicated their churches had a policy requiring performance evaluations to be conducted, 80 percent claimed to actually be doing it. Clearly, most of us believe that having an effective performance evaluation system is the proper thing to do (even if there is no written policy).

Beyond The Performance Review

To have a worthwhile performance management system, you must establish specific, realistic and measurable goals up front. Then spend most of your subsequent time helping your staff members monitor progress toward their goals in a helpful, coaching manner.

Then and only then have you set the stage to evaluate progress in a performance review. If you have done the first two steps well, your performance review should be a celebration for a job well done.[22]

17 Steps To Developing An Evaluation System

1. Answer these questions: Who will be evaluated? What method will be used? Who will do the evaluation? What are the standards used for comparison? Will the review lead to a promotion or raise? More assignments? More responsibility? More authority?

2. Allow employee ownership of the system by seeking employee input in the early stages of development.

3. Get the support of the ministerial staff, particularly the senior minister, Personnel Committee, and the vote of the church.

4. Define the purpose of each ministry.

5. Formulate goals.

6. Emphasize teamwork.

7. Review job descriptions; update and make corrections so they will lead to accomplishing ministry purpose.

8. Study available evaluation formats, then choose one or design a form to fit your need.

9. Give advance notice of review.

10. Arrange for a time without interruptions to conduct the review.

11. Be thorough and honest, but tactful and loving.

12. Praise where praise is due, coach or mentor when needed to correct problem areas.

13. Evaluate properly; not on personality but on performance. Focus on behavior (something tangible, provable) not on attitude.

14. Put the evaluation comments in writing, signed by both supervisor and employee.

15. Develop an action plan to correct mistakes and work on weak areas. Set a time for reevaluation.

16. Set goals and focus on ways to reach them before the next evaluation.

17. Follow-up actions, mentoring and coaching, should take place before next evaluation.

"Evaluation calls us to measure performance against purpose. Good evaluation demands that standards of effectiveness or success should be established beforehand. Goals always precede evaluation."[23]

Notes

[1] *Christian Leadership Letter*, World Vision, September 1985

[2] Marvin Myers, *Considerations for a Performance Review Plan*

[3] Al Cartwright, *Salary Administration*, NACBA, Fort Worth, p. 37

[4] James L. Murphy, *A Performance Appraisal Strategy*, National Institute in Church Finance and Administration, Atlanta, 1991, pp. 3–5

[5] James F. Hind, *The Heart and Soul of Effective Management*, Victor Books, Wheaton, IL, 1989, p. 19

[6] Ibid., p. 19

[7] Ibid., pp. 49, 53

[8] Ibid., pp. 53, 54, 62

[9] Louise C. Gee, *The Development of Job Desciptions and Performance Evaluations*, The National Institute in church Finance and Administration, Atlanta, 1990, pp. 4, 6

[10] Simeon May, *Performance Evaluations*, Southwestern Baptist Theological Seminary, Fort Worth, 1991, pp. iii–iv

[11] Edward R. Lycett, *Developing a Performance/Team Contribution Evaluation Procedure*, Southwestern Baptist Theological Seminary, Fort Worth, 1994, pp. 6–14

[12] George W. Sweeting, *Secrets of Excellence*, Moody Press, Chicago, p. 21

[13] Ibid., p. 13

[14] Ibid., p. 12

[15] Myron Rush, *Management: A Biblical Approach*, Victor Books, Wheaton, IL, p. 13

[16] Ibid., p. 5

[17] Tim J. Holcomb, *Personnel Administration Guide*, Convention Press, Nashville, 1988, p. 129

[18] May, p. 1

[19] Rush, p. 186

[20] Ibid.

[21] Judy R. Block, *Performance Appraisal on the Job: Making it Work*, Executive Enterprises Publications Co., New York, 1981, p. 20

[22] Dr. Ken Blanchard, "Managing Employees, Beyond the Performance Review," *Office Technology Management*

[23] Bruce P. Powers, *Church Administration Handbook*, Broadman, Nashville, 1985, p. 21

Chapter Three

REASONS FOR EMPLOYEE PERFORMANCE APPRAISALS

Many things can be gained from a performance analysis, evaluation, or appraisal. Performance standards should mean something to all concerned. Following are just some of the reasons to have a review and some benefits resulting from effective measurement of performance:

- Clarify goals
- Gain valuable insights
- Confirm priorities and objectives
- Increase communication
- Reduce anxiety
- Increase productivity
- Reinforce good work practices
- Provide guidance and direction
- Properly distribute workloads
- Remove surprises
- Measure performance
- Build team spirit
- Build support
- Restore broken relationships
- Improve performance
- Correct unsatisfactory job performance
- Relate individual performance to church goals

A good performance evaluation or appraisal system leaves both parties feeling they have gained something.

Does your church have the philosophy that there is no reason for a performance review if they can't give the employee a raise at the same time? If so, "you need to re-examine your thinking. Employees need to be told how well they are doing their jobs regardless of whether the church is in a position to give them a raise."[1]

Power

Common in the workplace today, even the church, is a power struggle between management and employee. Employers attempt to elicit performance based on authority and power. Even when employers do not intentionally seek to apply pressure, employees often perceive the power basis for the relationship and respond accordingly.

Paul Hersey and Ken Blanchard, in *Management of Organizational Behavior*, identify seven bases of power as having potential means of successfully influencing the behavior of others. They are defined as follows.

Coercive Power—based on fear.

Legitimate Power—based on the position held by the leader.

Expert Power—based on the leader's possession of expertise, skill and knowledge, which, through respect, influences others.

Reward Power—based on the leader's ability to provide rewards for other people who believe that compliance will lead to positive incentives such as pay, promotion or recognition.

Referent Power—based on the leader's personal traits.

Information Power—based on the leader's possession of our access to information that is perceived as valuable by others.

Connection Power—based on the leader's "connections" with influential or important persons inside or outside the organization.

K. R. Student studied the relationship of power to performance. Implicit in Student's conclusions is the contention that subordinates are more responsive to and satisfied with a leader whose influence attempts are not based entirely on position-based power (i.e., legitimate, reward, and coercive).

In those offices in which referent and expert power predominated, performance and satisfaction were high.[2]

Relationships/Group Goals

Generally, it is considered that the employer, the church, sets the goals and that employees are hired to help reach these goals. Employees, particularly church employees, by and large buy into the goals of the church when they seek employment in a church. This does not, however, eliminate their personal goals or their need for fulfillment. A good appraisal system can help merge the employee's personal goals with the group (church) goals.

From the beginning of time, individuals and groups have been dealing with the concept of team building, trying to establish a home, develop community or learn to work with each other. This is probably the most misunderstood concept in the area of staff relations. Most people believe just because they are on a church staff or part of a business relationship that they are a team. Most would accept the following definition, taken out of context, to be that of a team . . . "A team helps people accomplish more than they could working individually."[3]

The best definition I have found has been developed by the American Management Association. "The most distinguishing characteristic of a team is that its members have, as their highest priority, the accomplishment of team goals. They may be strong personalities, possess highly developed specialized skills and commit themselves to a variety of personal objectives they hope to achieve through their activity; but to them, the most important business at hand is the success of the group in reaching the goal that its members, collectively and with one voice, have set. The members support one another, collaborate freely, and communicate openly and clearly with one another."

Communication

Perception is important. Employees may incorrectly interpret information from employers if good communication lines are not established. Again, a good appraisal system can help in this area.

Steve Franklin in a lecture, "Interpersonal Communications," gave the following suggestions on communicating high expectations.

How to communicate high expectation:

1. Clear cut job descriptions.

2. Make truly participative decisions.

3. Personal praise for performance, not necessarily great performances. Praise the little things.

4. Let them do it with fear and trembling.

5. Show appreciation for uniqueness.[4]

Supervising Fellow Church Members

Some supervising principles are given by Robert D. Dale.[5] They are intended for persons working with church volunteers but are also appropriate for supervisor/employee relations. It displays love, dignity, and respect.

Supervision is actually more of a mentor-novice relationship.

Supervision blends learning by example, practice and feedback.

1. Pastors and other church staff ministers who supervise volunteer leaders and workers must be willing to put their ministry on display and allow others to look over their shoulders. The opportunity for novices to observe and question is an invaluable learning experience.

2. The practice of ministry is learning by doing. Much of it is "on-the-job" training. What's second nature to the veteran in ministry can be broken down into bite-sized chunks for the less experienced.

3. Feedback extends self-evaluation in objective, behavior-based change. Feedback allows failure to become a base for learning.

Effective supervisors affirm first then confront with caring directness.

Legal Aspects of Appraisal

A reality is that even though we are a church and are supposed to resolve our conflicts with law and justice, what seems just to one may appear unjust to another. A good appraisal system can help prevent unnecessary problems for the church.

A supervisor should carefully record any action taken to reprimand an employee and document the effort made to improve performance. This documented record should be placed in the employee's personnel file. It is helpful if the record also includes a signed statement by the employee acknowledging the agreement to improve performance. If repeated attempts to rectify the inadequate performance are not successful and termination becomes necessary, the records will provide sufficient information to indicate that the church was justified in its action. If a church does not follow such a process, there is a good possibility that an employee would have legal grounds for a lawsuit.[6]

Julie Bloss gives the following legal reason for honest evaluations.

Performance reviews are worthless if the supervisor does not rate employees honestly. Because of fear of confrontation, supervisors may tend to inflate performance reviews. That's not fair to the employer or employee. If an employee is having performance problems, those should be addressed. Employers who give employees good performance reviews and then decide to terminate them for poor job performance are setting themselves up for legal trouble. Of course, it is possible that an employee's performance can deteriorate after a review, and those cases will have to be dealt with individually.[7]

Quality Work

A detour is never pleasant. It takes an employee off the track to his or her destination, uses time, and adds to frustration.

When you're driving your car, a roadblock is easy to spot; you can identify it from a mile off on a clear day. Sometimes a roadblock that takes someone away from working goals is harder to see.

In his book *Out of Crisis*, Edward Deming details 14 steps to quality. His work helps anyone to identify progress-blocking conditions that exist on the job. For example:

- **The missing commitment:** It's a barrier that blocks the path to consistent quality. Challenge employees to break it down by deciding to improve, constantly and forever, every step of the way. Little things count tremendously and build throughout their work. Maybe the first step will be getting a good night's sleep so you will arrive in a bright, alert frame of mind.

- **Barriers between employee and other staff members:** This roadblock can cause lost messages, unnecessary work and stress that takes the joy out of life and threatens quality. If you or another employee feel separated from others, do whatever is necessary to improve communication. If the barrier seems to be the result of some procedure, suggest changes. Think about it.

- **The missing skill:** Do employees really know everything that will make machines or computers as effective as they could be? A missing area of skill that would make a job easier has a bearing on the quality of the work produced. Ask questions, lead employees to sign up for advanced training or to study manuals to find out all they can about the equipment.

- **Fear:** It shouldn't exist in productive people. Fear is a barrier to quality because it robs people of pride of workmanship. Blast this roadblock to progress by having a talk with your supervisor or employees. If employees have the commitment and are developing their skills, they can erase fear and stay on the road to consistent quality in their work.

Deming says everyone in an organization should be striving to accomplish the goal of improved work and service quality. He's right, of course. If you find your path is blocked by these or other barriers, do what you must to blast them away.

An honest performance evaluation is a good tool to learn about and blast away the roadblocks detouring your staff from quality workmanship.

For we are his workmanship, created in Christ Jesus unto good works, which God hath before ordained that we should walk in them.

Ephesians 2:10 KJV

What Makes an Employee Promotable?

How do you spot an employee eligible for advancement? Here are a few qualities to look for:

1. **Initiative**—Presents solutions, not problems.

2. **Imagination**—Figures out better ways to do the job.

3. **Self-reliance**—Knows that one's success and advancement will be determined by one's own performance and energy.

4. **Responsibility**—Enjoys and is willing to accept challenges.

5. **Perseverance**—Is not discouraged by obstacles, but determined to get the job done in spite of them. Morale. Has a positive attitude toward his job and fellow employees.

6. **Industriousness**—Always puts in a full day's work, utilizing time effectively.

Notes

1 Julie Bloss, *The Church Guide to Employment Law*, Matthews, NC, Christian Ministry Resources, 1993, p. 120

2 Myron Rush, *Management: A Biblical Approach*, Victor Books, 1990, p. 48

3 Paul Hersey and Ken Blanchard, *Management of Organizational Behavior*, Prentice-Hall, Inc., Englewood Cliffs, NJ, 1982, pp. 178–179

4 Steve Franklin, "Interpersonal Communications," lecture at the National Institute in Church Finance and Administration at Candler School of Theology, Atlanta, April 1988

5 "Working with People," *Church Administration Handbook*, edited by Bruce P. Powers, Broadman, Nashville, TN 1985, p. 75

6 Ibid., p. 238

7 Bloss, p. 120

Chapter Four

WHO SHOULD EVALUATE?

By Simeon May, FCBA

In the church there are five possible parties who could perform the evaluation:

1. Supervisor

2. Self

3. Peers

4. Subordinates

5. Church members

The factors used to determine which party or parties qualify to perform the evaluation are:

- Awareness of the objectives of the employee's job.

- Frequent observation of the employee on the job.

- Capability to determine whether the established standards are being met.[1]

Supervisor

The supervisory evaluation is the most common and the one that most obviously meets the qualifications. If a supervisor is doing his job properly, he will certainly be aware of the employee's job objectives (hopefully having worked with the employee to establish the expectations), and he will be frequently observing the employee on the job.

Self

An employee can be expected to enter the evaluation session with some preconceptions as to how he is performing; therefore, self-evaluation is inevitable. The disagreements which arise from the evaluation by the supervisor and the evaluation by the employee form the basis for meaningful discussions and development.[2]

Sometimes there is a reluctance on the part of the employee to discuss his performance. When some type of evaluation form is used, the supervisor might require the employee to complete the form as a self-evaluation. A comparison of the supervisor's and the employee's evaluation forms could then be the "ice- breaker" for the employee and open up constructive dialogue.

Peers

A confidential peer evaluation can be used by the supervisor to gain an understanding of how the employee is perceived by the people with whom the employee works side-by-side. A single supervisor may not be able to observe everything an employee does. By using the peer evaluation, the supervisor may discover areas of concern, as observed by the peer group, which he has not observed.

A non-confidential peer evaluation is used most frequently in highly professional organizations, such as professors in universities or physicians in clinics.[3] For this peer evaluation to be effective, there must exist a high level of interpersonal trust. In the church context, there must be a commitment to shared ministry and teamwork.[4] Using this setting (such as a weekly staff meeting or a less frequent staff retreat), mutual expectations, task interdependencies and team goals are discussed in an open format.

Subordinates

The formal evaluation of a superior by his subordinates is certainly out of the ordinary. However, the use of the subordinate evaluation could provide a superior's supervisor with some insight as to the superior's behavior. Also, knowing how one is perceived by his subordinates can be an important ingredient in the change of a superior's behavior.[5] One pastor stated, "I would not be opposed to being [evaluated] in my performance by the Executive Staff—Minister of Music, Minister of Education, and Church Administrator."

Church Members

Selected groups or individuals from the congregation can be used effectively in the evaluation process. The supervisor may discover that while the subordinate is performing in the manner the supervisor expects, the subordinate may not be acting in a manner expected by the lay person.

The pastor and/or personnel committee could select the persons to be involved in the process. Of course these "lay evaluators" must meet the qualifications for evaluation as listed earlier—they must understand the expectations for the employee and be a frequent observer of the employee.

The use of more than one group or individual may be required. For example, the chair of the finance committee may be qualified to evaluate the CBA on financial matters, but is probably not qualified to evaluate the CBA on property issues.

In response to my questionnaire, several pastors indicated that the pastor should not be evaluated, one even stating that "no one was qualified." However, most of the pastors felt they should be evaluated. In many cases, the evaluators are the members of the personnel committee. In a few instances, the evaluators are the chair of the deacons, the chair of the personnel committee, and the chair of the finance committee. This last scenario is included in the bylaws of my church. In addition, my pastor meets regularly with the four most recent chairs of the deacons.

Notes

[1] Gary P. Latham and Kenneth N. Wexley, *Increasing Productivity Through Performance Appraisal*, Addison-Wesley, Reading, MA, 1981, p. 83

[2] L.L. Cummings and Donald P. Schwab, "Who Evaluates?" in *The Performance Appraisal Sourcebook*, Lloyd S. Baird, Richard W. Beatty, and Craig Eric Schneier, (eds), Human Resource Development Press, Amherst, MA, 1982, p. 93

[3] Ibid., p. 82

[4] Bill Caldwell, "Measuring Performance," in *Personnel Administration Guide for Southern Baptist Churches* compiled by Tim J. Holcomb, Convention Press, Nashville, 1988, p. 142

[5] Cummings, p. 83

Chapter Five

WHEN TO EVALUATE

By Simeon May, FCBA

There are two questions regarding when to conduct a performance evaluation:

1. whether to conduct appraisals as needed or to conduct only formal appraisals at a specified time or times during the year, and

2. whether or not to conduct appraisals in conjunction with salary reviews.

Frequency

In regard to the frequency of feedback, experts concur that problems should be resolved as they arise. Problems should never be left to accumulate until emotions take charge.[1] H. John Bernardin cited a study in which the respondents "preferred more frequent feedback given on an informal, on-the-job basis rather than just after an appraisal period. Few respondents felt formal appraisals were the most useful means for feedback."[2]

If a change of behavior is the purpose of the evaluation, then it must be conducted frequently with explicit feedback and setting specific goals. The actions which an employee needs to stop, start or continue must be specified on an ongoing basis.[3]

Salary Reviews

Opinions are split on whether to conduct performance evaluations in conjunction with salary reviews. Seventy-two percent of the survey respondents indicated that performance evaluations were conducted in conjunction with salary reviews. The primary advantage of separating the two is that during a performance evaluation the discussion deals with performance only. This allows the supervisor to objectively assess the employee without dealing with the emotionally charged issue of pay. In determining a salary increase, M. E. Schnake submits that "a supervisor must consider, among other things, how the employee's pay compares with the pay of other employees in his or her department, the employee's 'market value' outside the company,

education and job experience, seniority, and any restrictive wage guidelines in place."[4]

Nevertheless, if the church desires to give salary increases based on merit, the performance evaluation is the tool for this purpose. Also, in order for the merit pay system to be equitable to all employees, the evaluations must be conducted on an "apples to apples" basis by all supervisors within classes of employment. For example, a minister of education evaluating his minister of youth must have the same understanding of the meaning of the ratings as the minister of music evaluating the associate minister of music.

Five Essentials Of A Good Job Description

1. **Function**—Why the job exists, or the general purpose it serves the organization as a whole.

2. **Authority**—What the individual is specifically authorized to do and to decide, the positions that report to this individual, and the boundaries within which this individual may act freely.

3. **Responsibility**—The specific areas of activity in which this individual is responsible for results, and the general kind of results expected of this individual.

4. **Reportability**—When, how and to whom this individual must report.

5. **Accountability**—State of being answerable, subject to a statement of reasons, causes, results, conduct or action.

Notes

1   Charles A. Tidwell, *Church Administration Effective Leadership for Ministry*, Broadman Press, Nashville, 1985, p. 249

2   John Bernardin in *Performance Assessment—Methods & Applications*, Ronald A. Berk, (ed), The Johns Hopkins University Press, Baltimore, 1986, p. 280

3   Gary P. Latham and Kenneth N. Wesley, *Increasing Productivity Through Performance Appraisal*, Addison-Wesley, Reading, PA, 1981, p. 150

4   M.E. Schnake, "Apples and Oranges: Salary Review and Performance Review," *Supervisory Management*, November 1980, pp. 32–34

Chapter Six

JOB DESCRIPTIONS

The first step in any effort to measure performance is to know what the job is supposed to include.[1] This is generally determined with a *job description.*

"Job descriptions serve four main purposes:

- To give an overall concept of the tasks performed in each position.

- To show how each job differs from the others.

- To identify the job qualifications required to perform each job.

- To provide an objective method to determine each job's relative worth when compared to other jobs."[2]

Job descriptions make it possible to present a great deal of organized, pertinent information about each position, whether as part of an employment manual, as a part of the employment interview or as a basis for a performance review or appraisal.

The central problem of personnel administration is to induce a group of people—each with individual needs and personality—to work together for the objectives of the organization;[3] hence the need to have strong up-to-date and effective job descriptions. Written correctly, with input, these can also lead to strong performance expectations.

In beginning the development of job descriptions, we need to establish a clear understanding of their value. Some of the benefits derived from a job description are:

1. To confirm our common, shared mission and our major priorities and objectives.

2. To give guidance and direction. A staff member can function more efficiently with less supervision.

3. To act as an aid for properly distributing work loads.

4. To help in measuring work performance. If there is no job description, there can be no basis for job evaluations.

5. To contribute to morale by building support between the individual, the staff-parish relations committee and the total church. This can be likened to a circle of support that passes freely among those involved.

6. It can serve as the basis for interviewing new personnel. It simply communicates what services are desired by the church.[4]

"A written job description is an organized summary of the duties, tasks, responsibilities, and accountability involved in a staff position."[5]

Job descriptions won't help if they are inaccurate, incomplete or out-of-date.

Alvin Lewis writing in *The Clergy Journal* lists eight components that should be included in each job description.

1. **Date**—Each job description should be considered a living document that can change and grow over the years. Therefore, each should be dated to help identify the most current.

2. **Title**—Each should include a position title that is brief but descriptive.

3. **Purpose**—The purpose identifies the "why" of the position by stating what is to be accomplished.

4. **Duties and Responsibilities**—This describes the "how" of the job by giving some details of the task.

5. **Working Relationships**—Each staff member should know to whom he or she is accountable.

6. **Education and Experience**—Are there special degrees or training required for this position?

7. **Spiritual Requirements**—Unlike secular employment, the church can detail the spiritual requirements for a job.[6]

Job descriptions are the background to which performance must be compared.

A good job description will define responsibilities and contain a listing of duties to be performed. This list then becomes the criteria against which a person's performance can be measured.

> **Job descriptions are the background to which performance must be compared.**

Seventeen percent of the respondents in a survey conducted for this project said they did not refer to job descriptions when conducting performance evaluation. One CBA stated "It is usually out-of-date or different to the actual job assignment."

Job descriptions must be maintained in order for them to be used effectively in the evaluation process. An up-to-date accurate job description not only helps the boss and the subordinate know what is expected but helps others also know what they are doing and why.

Olan Hendrix states a job description is antiquated "if it has not been reviewed with the people concerned, the boss and the subordinate, at least once a year, up-dated, retyped, and re-issued."[7]

A pastor, who does not refer to job descriptions said, "We have a good understanding of responsibilities." I'm not sure who the "we" is, and wonder if the staff and laymen would be in agreement with him.

A CBA stated it well, "Performance cannot be evaluated abstractly. It must be done in light of the tasks and work to be completed. Job descriptions are the background to which performance must be compared."

Job descriptions for secretarial/clerical positions are rather easy to write and maintain due to their technical nature. Job descriptions for the ministerial staff, where innovation, creativity and imagination are involved, are more difficult to write, but are more important due to the managerial nature of the tasks.[8]

People like to live up to what is expected of them. It is a universal desire of employees to want to know what is expected of them and how well they are meeting those expectations. This entails performance appraisal. If praise is desired and given or if shortcomings are pointed out, when they exist, the net effect is to alter people's behavior to some degree. Furthermore, performance appraisal is an important aspect of the effective utilization of human resources.

In any enterprise, the performance appraisal can be viewed as an inventory of employees. It should be viewed as an orderly effort that is designed to improve the relationship between the supervisor and the staff person and to help the staff person achieve self-improvement and progress. The aim of performance appraisal is to achieve a two-way understanding, which includes the mutual agreement of objectives and the development of plans and the means of self improvement.[9]

Mutual understanding and agreement on duties and responsibilities (the job description) are essential to the job evaluation and performance appraisal processes. All too often an employee is hired to perform in one capacity and finds the position evolving into something much bigger because of that employee's capabilities. Without some form of control, preferably through the job description, employees can become quite disenchanted. Communication to the employee about his or her role in the organization is a must.[10]

Surely there is no question that job descriptions can be useful for a wide range of purposes. To be of maximum use, they must be widely distributed. Employees and supervisors alike should know that they exist and that continual updating makes them viable.

Job descriptions can be a big help or they can be a complete waste of time. They won't help if they are inaccurate, incomplete or out-of-date. Nor will the descriptions help if employees become distrustful of them or misunderstand their purpose. To be helpful, job descriptions must cover every position in the (church). They must present an operational view of the whole works; they must show that each and every job in the (church) has been designed to fit together like the spokes of a wheel.

The useful job description has these qualities:

• It is up-to-date

• The job title fits

• The job summary gives a bird's-eye view of the most important responsibilities

• Relationships and responsibilities for coordinating with other people are clearly and comprehensively stated

• Duties are stated concisely

The description tells the employee what one should know about the job and what he or she is responsible for. In the last analysis, a job description is a key communication between supervisor and employee. Each employee, with an appropriate job description, can better work toward overall (church) goals.[11]

Value of Job Descriptions

The value of church job descriptions was almost forced upon me when I attended the 1989 Summer Seminar of the National Institute in Church Finance and Administration at Candler School of Theology. The first day was spent in getting acquainted with our fellow classmates, and I heard story after story of church staffs that are in turmoil. None of these churches had job descriptions and each staff person seemed to go his or her way without regard for any of the other staff members. The people felt no direction or support in their situation.

The Staff as a Team

I can think of no other work place where it is so imperative that the staff be a team as in a church. Robert Greenleaf states in *Servant Leadership* that the alienated and purposeless have multiplied while churches grope for a way to serve. He believes that the staff of an institution (church) should be set up "Primus Inter Pares"—first among equals. We all are at one time leaders in our job situations and at other time servants. We serve through leading, and we lead by serving.[12]

"Servant leaders are healers in the sense of making whole by helping others to see a larger and nobler vision, a purpose, than they would be likely to attain for themselves."[13]

What a beautiful attainment for a church staff to work in this kind of environment rather than the chaos and pettiness that seem to exist on some church staffs. *The Church Administration Handbook* states "The staff members should form a cohesive whole which is greater than the sum of its parts."[14]

"The writing of job descriptions is an indication to staff members of interest in them and their work. It supports efficient organization and the concept of the staff as a team."[15]

A Helpful Tool

One purpose of job descriptions is to stimulate and grow the personnel of the church.

Personnel management is relatively new as a science, but its basic philosophy was created in the Golden Rule.

Every church has job descriptions of some sort. They may be written, or they may exist only in someone's mind. When unwritten, a staff member may not be sure of his exact responsibilities. New assignments added from time to time may have expanded his job during the years. Written job descriptions identify responsibility.

Job descriptions serve:

• To identify the job qualifications required to perform each job.

• To prevent misunderstandings and create a feeling of trust and mutual concern.[16]

• To make it possible to present a great deal of organized, pertinent information about each position quickly and concisely.[17]

- To provide a tool by which (church) objectives are broken down into smaller segments, and by which responsibility for achieving those goals is delegated throughout the organization.[18]

Carefully prepared, properly used job descriptions can be valuable to the individuals in an organization. Organizations require division of responsibility. As more and more people are added to the organization, the division becomes greater. Division and delegation of authority to make decisions help decentralize and give added responsibility and authority to more individuals. It emphasizes the need for clearer definitions of functions, responsibilities, authority, relationships and accountability of each position.

Job descriptions have several (additional) important advantages:

- They help the manager analyze and improve organization structure, and see whether all company responsibilities are fully covered.

- Job descriptions explain and clarify who is responsible for what within the organization and help record relationships between individuals.

- Job descriptions help the person in the job understand the ramifications of the position. The employee can more accurately analyze and assess the relative importance of everything for which they are held accountable.

- Job descriptions are helpful to job applicants, to employees and to supervisors at every stage in the employment relationship.

- Job descriptions play a role in personnel development and performance appraisal.

- A job description is fundamental to job evaluation as well as being an integral part of a sound wage and salary program.

- Accurate, comprehensive job descriptions form a factual basis for making wage and salary surveys, grading jobs and developing a fair wage and salary structure.

- Job descriptions show us what we are supposed to do and show our supervisor what we are doing.

A Guide

A job description must be recognized for what it is—a description, a guide, not an inflexible standard to be followed slavishly. It has limitations and must be constantly restudied and, if necessary, adapted to new needs and changing situations and different personalities. While reasonable uniformity may be desirable in some situations, in others, management needs to be flexible. This flexibility encourages managers to think creatively about the whole range of job-person relationships. There is the possibility of a number of alternative "clusterings" of duties to assist in the matching of people and jobs.[19]

Job descriptions are prepared after careful observation of the work performed, careful study of the job requirements, and careful discussion with present employees.[20]

The following steps are suggested as a church considers writing job descriptions:

Decide to do it. The pastor, administrator, and the personnel committee should give leadership to the project.

Agree on the work scope of the job descriptions. Subcommittees might address these tasks: 1) determine the method of securing job information from the workers; 2) design the job questionnaire and job description forms; 3) analyze the completed questionnaires for clarity, completeness and correctness; 4) write the job descriptions; and 5) assist in implementing the project.

Conduct conferences with the staff members, explaining the purpose of the project. Distribute and explain copies of the questionnaire to the workers during this conference.

Follow these five rules for securing information for job descriptions:

1. The employee should understand that the job, not the person, is being described.

2. The interviewer should have a persuasive and reassuring manner, remembering that the employee is a human being whose job is important to him or her.

3. It is best to let the employee describe the job.

4. The interviewer shouldn't put words into the employee's mouth but should guide the discussion and avoid too many digressions.

5. The employee shouldn't be given the impression that the interview is being rushed or that what he or she considers valuable is being discounted.

In sum, serious, courteous, thorough, objective and efficient interviews will yield the most useful information for preparing job descriptions for all levels of employees.[21]

The well-written job description contains short, factual statements that minimize the need for interpretation. A job description should be written in clear, concise, easy-to-understand language that accurately describes the job.

The format of the job description should be organized to facilitate both a quick understanding on the reader's part and the extraction of needed information. The job being described should be positively identified by a meaningful job title that reflects the job duties and responsibilities.

Basic Parts of a Job Description

The **job title** should be as descriptive as possible of the work that is accomplished by this position.

The **level of the job in the organization** should be indicated by identifying the position to which it reports and the position it supervises.

The **purpose of the job** and a summary of its duties should be noted in two or three brief sentences.

Finally, the **major duties and responsibilities** should be listed.

The job description is not a step-by-step account of the way a job is done but is a summary with enough information to assure that the job can be accurately evaluated and rated.

Summary

- Summarize the duties and responsibilities of each position.

- Use language that is specific, avoiding general terms—"handle," "responsible for"—which make it difficult to know just what is meant. The wording should convey one definite meaning—"file," "supervise," "maintain"—and not several possible meanings.

- Use the present tense.

- Accuracy is of utmost importance.

- Reach an agreement between supervisors and workers in wording of job descriptions, making sure information is up-to-date and correct.

The finished product will be meaningful and one in which all involved can take pride.[22]

The job description tells the employee what one should know about the job and the responsibilities related to it. In the last analysis, a job description is a key communication between supervisor and employee. Employees, with appropriate job descriptions, can better work toward overall (church) goals.[23]

Notes

1   Tim J. Holcomb, *Personnel Administration Guide for Southern Baptist Churches*, Nashville, Convention Press, 1988, p. 131

2   *Church Staff Administration: Practical Approaches*, Leonard E. Wedel, Broadman Press, Nashville, p. 54

3   Ibid., p. 191

4   Lucy R. Hopkins, "Why Have A Job Description?," *Church Administration*, Nashville, February 1977, p. 41

5   *Guidelines for Developing Church Job Descriptions*, Division of Diaconal Ministry, Board of Higher Education and Ministry, The United Methodist Church, Nashville, October 1988

6   Alvin Lewis, "How About A Job Description?," *Church Management: The Clergy Journal*, May/June, 1980, p. 58

7   Olan Hendrix, *Management for the Christian Lead*, Mott Media, Milford, MI, 1981, p. 87

8   Ibid., p. 88

9   Terry and Stallard, *Office Mangement and Control*, Richard D. Irwin, p. 409

10 John D. Ulery, *Job Descriptions In Manufacturing Industries*, AMA, 1981, p. 3

11 Joseph J. Famularo, *Organizational Planning Manual*, AMA, 1979, p. 194

12 Robert K. Geeenleaf, *Servant Leadership*, Paulist Press, New York, 1977, p. 13

13 Ibid., p. 227

14 Bruce P. Powers, *Church Administration Handbook*, Broadman Press, Nashville, 1985, p. 94

15 *Guidelines for Developing Church Job Descriptions*, Division of Diaconal Ministry, Board of Higher Education and Ministry, The United Methodist Church, Nashville, October 1988

16 Robert A. Young, *The Development of a Church Manual of Administrative Policies*, Bel-Air Church Directory Publishers, Inc., 1975, p. 11

17 Leonard W. Wedel, CSA, *Church Staff Administration—Practical Approaches*, Broadman Press, Nashville, 1978, p. 54

18 Gordon Evans, *Managerial Job Descriptions in Manufacturing*, AMA, 1974, p. 54

19 George Strauss and Leonard R. Sayles, *Personnel—The Human Problems of Management*, Prentice-Hall, Inc., Englewood Cliffs, NJ, 1972, p. 382

20 H. Webster Johnson and William G. Savage, *Administrative Office Mangement*, Addision-Wesley, Reading, PA, 1968, p. 542

21 Joseph J. Famularo, *Organizational Planning Manual*, Prentice-Hall, Inc., Englewood Cliffs, NJ, 1964, p. 191

22 John D. Ulery, *Job Descriptions in Manufacturing Industries*, AMA, 1981, p. 6

23 Joseph J. Famularo, *Organizational Planning Manual*, Prentice-Hall, Inc., Englewood Cliffs, NJ, 1964, p. 194

FACTORS FOR EFFECTIVE PERFORMANCE

People work better when they know:

1. **What they are expected to do**.

2. **What is their scope of authority**.

3. **What the standards are for a job well done**.

4. **Where they are falling short**.

5. **To whom they are responsible**.

6. **What are the rewards for good work**.

7. **That interest is shown in their success and future**.

A church should have answers for the questions asked in this section. These questions may be answered by the pastor and/or the personnel committee members or whoever is interviewing a prospective ministerial or support staff member.

1. **What am I supposed to do?**—This question shows the need for a workable job description. A church is not ready to call a staff member until it can specify what that member's work will be.

2. **What is my scope of authority?**—Can I dismiss a secretary? Can I employ or replace service personnel, and if so, for what reasons? Are there guidelines for spending budget monies? If so, what are they? What relationship do I have with other staff members, the nominating committee and other committees?

3. **What are the standards for a job well done?**—How will I know when I am doing good work? By what performance standards can I measure my ministry's progress? Any standard should be established with the objectives and priorities of the church's program in mind.

4. **Where am I falling short?**—Will I have regular performance reviews? Regular performance reviews let a staff member know where he stands. If the personnel committee only confers with an employee when there is something wrong, it is poor or negative supervision.

5. **To whom am I responsible?**—It is discouraging never to understand who one's immediate supervisor is. Is it the pastor, the personnel committee, the church?

6. **What are the rewards for good work?**—The tangible rewards should be stated in the policies of a church. Merited praise is always a motivating reward. A church may need to do additional planning in the area of rewards for staff members.

7. **Will the pastor or my supervisor be interested in my success and future?**—Having one's supervisor and other staff members interested in one's success and future builds trust and affirms one's ministry.

Chapter Seven

JOB STANDARDS

A step beyond the writing of job descriptions is the establishment of performance standards. If a supervisor is going to communicate appreciation and/or criticism to a subordinate, it must be done on the basis of the subordinate's expectations. Often, it is assumed the employee understands what is expected, or that the employee will develop an understanding on his own.[1] Myron Rush states that "unless performance standards are clearly defined, with measurable terminology, employees have no way of knowing what is expected of them."[2]

Bill Caldwell defines performance standards as "statements of observable conditions which will exist when a job has been well done."[3] People like to meet expectations but are discouraged if they are evaluated against some measure that was unknown to them in advance. Telling employees how, why and when keeps expectations clear. A specific due date or a budget are items which cannot be misunderstood. Also, the setting of performance standards keeps evaluation sessions from becoming subjective.

If a minister of education is expected to establish a new Bible study group, he must not be judged by how many people attend. To be evaluated on the basis of attendance, he would have to be able to control the weather, sports schedules, family circumstances and a person's available time. What he can control is the location, the selection and training of a teacher, the selection of literature and the promotion of the study.

Whether we like it or not, every job has some type of performance expectation. When we place that in the Christian perspective, we realize that, *"God is performance conscious.* Scripture indicates His concern about the quality and level of our work performance by saying, *'Work hard and cheerfully at all you do, just as though you were working for the Lord and not merely for your masters'* (Col. 3:23, LB). While on earth, Jesus apparently performed to the best of His ability for those observing His actions commented, *'He has done everything well'* (Mark 7:37)."[4]

Performance standards should mean something to all concerned. "A philosophy should also be built on certain benefits that will result from effective measurement of performance. A church can expect some or all of the following benefits to be achieved.

- Measuring and judging performance of personnel from an objective viewpoint

- Relating individual performance to church goals

- Clarifying both the job to be done and the expectations of the accomplishments of the job

- Facilitating the competence and growth of personnel

- Improving communication between supervisors and employees

- Providing recognition commensurate with results

- Stimulating motivation of personnel

- Providing a process for organization control

- Identifying common training and educational needs of personnel

- Providing a means of measuring supervisors

In addition the individuals who work for the church can expect certain benefits to be achieved:

- Knowing how well they are doing in the performance

- Knowing better what they are supposed to be doing

- Identifying priorities more clearly

- Providing development and growth opportunities

- Providing better relationship with supervisors

- Providing a more objective basis for decisions about promotion, compensations, etc."[5]

In dealing with the area of performance standards, a common language needs to be developed between supervisors in the same organization (or church) to provide consistency.

An overall plan should be developed by and for the organization to aid in this process. What is *"Outstanding Work,"* what is deemed to be *"Satisfactory"* and in keeping with the church's expectations of it's ministry and staff, and what is to be considered as *"Unsatisfactory"*? These issues need to be settled before the process begins.

As well as setting performance standards, goals should also be set jointly between the supervisor and the employee. There is a difference between goals and standards. "A **goal** is a **statement** of results which are to be achieved. Goals describe:

1. conditions that will exist when the desired outcome has been accomplished;

2. a time frame during which the outcome is to be completed;

3. resources the organization is willing to commit in order to achieve the desired result.

Goals should be challenging, but achievable and established with the participation of those responsible for meeting them.

A **standard** refers to an ongoing performance criteria that must be met time and time again."[6]

The first portion of one appraisal system is the appraisal based on the standard of performance. Each position description has three basic parts. One is the responsibility section, which is a listing of the major duties of the staff member.

The second is the goals section. Each responsibility and goal is a standard of performance expressed in past tense. For instance, if a responsibility of the minister of music is "To show consistent enrollment growth in all choirs," then the goal could be expressed as, "To show consistent enrollment growth in all choirs." Thus, a standard of performance could be, "When a twenty percent gain in enrollment in the total choir program is realized." This is a standard of performance expressed in past tense. That is, the goal has been met when this standard has been achieved.

During the appraisal interview with the minister of music, the pastor (superior) will ask five questions about each of his standards of performance. These questions are:

1. How successful were you in achieving this standard of performance?

2. Are you pleased with this degree of success?

3. What problems did you encounter in meeting this standard?

4. What new insights of knowledge did you gain in working toward this standard?

5. Do you plan to re-enter this item as a standard of performance during the next appraisal period?

Thus, in this fashion the standard of performance becomes one phase of the total appraisal system.[7]

Bill Caldwell gives this format for writing performance standards. "A format for writing performance standards should be used. Consider the following:

Duty	Purpose(s)	Standards
The worker does these things	*for these reasons*	*as evidenced by these conditions*
worker + verb + object	in order to/that	performance is satisfactory when

If this or a similar format is used, looking at each duty on a job description and indicating the standard is simple. For some duties, the Purpose(s) section might be self-explanatory and, therefore, not needed. Focusing on what the purpose is in attempting to identify the standards is a helpful part of the process.

Duty	Purpose(s)	Standards
A minister visits hospitals	to express care for the sick	by seeing every church member admitted **or** by seeing each member hospitalized on my assigned day **or** by seeing each person who has no church affiliation.

"Following a simple format will enable supervisors and workers to agree on ways in which the performance can be analyzed with a view toward improving the work. Performance expectations must be developed and accepted by all before measurement can be effective."[8]

Notes

[1] Ted W. Engstrom and Edward R. Dayton, *The Art of Management for Christian Leaders*, Zondervan Publishing House, Grand Rapids, MI, 1989, p. 162

[2] Myron Rush, *Management: A Biblical Approach*, Victor Books, Wheaton, IL, 1983, p. 186

[3] Bill Caldwell, "Measuring Performance," in *Personal Administration Guide For Southern Baptist Churches*, compiled by Tim J. Holcomb, Convention Press, Nashville, 1988, p. 132

[4] Rush, p. 187

[5] Caldwell, p. 130

[6] Robert B. Maddux, *Effective Performance Appraisals*, Crisp Publications, Inc., Los Altos, CA, 1987, p. 15

[7] Jerry M. Poteet, "Church Staff Performance Reviews/Appraisals," *Church Administration*, Nashville, July 1981, pp. 14–16

[8] Caldwell, pp. 131–132

THE EMPLOYEE PERFORMANCE REVIEW

I. Setting Performance Goals

1. Review job description
2. Review annual plans
3. Consider special projects
4. Identify expected key results
5. Participatively establish goals with standards that specify: what is to be done, when, how much, how many, how well, with what resources
6. Goals should be: significant, challenging, specific, measurable, understandable, attainable, results-oriented, job-related
7. Identify criteria for current performance level and next performance level
8. Weight standards according to relative importance
9. Share copies with employee, supervisor, next level of supervision

II. Preparing For Performance Review

1. Schedule review in advance
2. Provide for privacy, comfort, communication
3. Ask employee to complete forms, bring to review
4. Review data from reports, accomplishments, feedback
5. Complete forms
6. Analyze review to ensure: fairness, consistency, equity, legality, objectivity, explainability

III. Conducting Performance Review

1. State purpose of review
2. Establish communication climate
3. Review employee's completed forms
4. Discuss goals achieved, affirming praiseworthy performance
5. Review performance on additional assignments completed
6. Assess performance on goals not achieved; explore problems
7. Recognize potential and strengths, citing examples
8. Identify and provide written documentation for performance problems
9. Explore career aspirations
10. Decide upon development plans
11. Elicit feedback on supervisory style
12. Restate main points of review
13. Date forms and secure signatures, indicating discussion has taken place
14. Communicate salary decision
15. Set and clarify goals and standards for next review period

Chapter Eight
THE PERFORMANCE EVALUATION INTERVIEW

The performance evaluation process is not completed until some type of closure comes to the project. This is generally known as the performance evaluation interview or the evaluation session. "The evaluation session is an excellent vehicle for demonstrating to employees that management is committed to meeting their work-related needs. It also gives the supervisor a chance to establish a trust relationship with his subordinates. In addition, it becomes the setting for delegating decision-making power to employees and helping them turn failures and mistakes into learning experiences. It is a time, too, when the employee receives positive recognition for work accomplished and constructive criticism as needed."[1] Not always wanted by either party, "the employee (however) has a legitimate need to know how his performance compares with his supervisor's expectations."[2]

The performance evaluation/appraisal interview should have three objectives:

1. To learn what employees think of their own performance and what their primary motivations are.

2. To give your own assessment of what the employee has accomplished. This gives a forum for the supervisor to give praise for good performance so it will continue and to call attention for needed improvement.

3. To make plans for future good performance.

So, the performance evaluation interview is an important element in the process.

Prepare For A Successful Evaluation Interview

Interviewing is always an important task, whether it comes during the interview process on a yearly basis, such as the performance evaluation process, or when a person exits.

The supervisor who accepts or is assigned the role of interviewer, must develop some basic skills in interviewing. This is mandatory! Some individuals tend to be very successful at the task of interviewing, while most tend to feel like failures. If we view any type of interview as "just something we have to do, and must fit it into our schedule," then we are setting ourselves and the person to be interviewed up for failure. Any person preparing for an interview should evaluate their own skills before they proceed. In preparing for a successful performance evaluation interview:

- Do a thorough analysis of the job requirements in advance.

- Compare job qualifications on the application (or with the existing file) with the job requirements, prior to the interview.

- Develop a logical plan in advance based on information required to make a selection decision (or plan for improvement).

- Get applicants to talk freely, and listen while they do so.

- Evaluate the facts, and avoid premature conclusions and stereotyping.

- Adhere to equal employment opportunity guidelines.[3]

Prior to conducting a performance appraisal, identify and develop items to be covered. Since employee performance in the current job is the central issue, gather relevant data concerning job requirements and the established goals or standards. Next, assess the employee's performance on the above for the appraisal period. Then:

- Review the job requirements to be sure you are fully conversant with them.

- Review the goals and standards you previously agreed upon with the employee plus any notes you have relating to their achievement.

- Review the employee's history including:
  - job skills
  - training
  - experience
  - special or unique qualifications
  - past jobs and job performance

- Evaluate job performance versus job expectations for the period being appraised, and rate it from unacceptable to outstanding.

- Note any variances in the employee's performance that need to be discussed. Provide specific examples.

- Consider career opportunities or limitations for this person. Be prepared to discuss them.[4]

Robert Maddux gives several types of interviews including the businesslike interview. He suggests the businesslike interview is the best format in which to prepare and conduct the interview of the performance appraisal. He defines the businesslike interview as: "a social situation with a business purpose in which worthwhile information is exchanged between parties."[5]

While there are no set rules, it is generally agreed that the proper setting for the appraisal interview is private, without distractions or interruptions, and informal.[6]

There are many dynamics that take place during the interview. Believing that all employees have a basic need to do their best, they may dread the evaluation process, especially the interview. "Unsatisfactory performance may mean being fired, facing embar-

rassing and irritating criticism, or having to undergo painful behavioral changes. But the employee's need to know how he is doing is more important than the fear of finding out, and most employees are better off knowing than not knowing."[7]

Develop a Two-Way Learning Environment

If the interview is successful, the supervisor should work on developing a two-way learning environment, for the one being interviewed and for himself. "If the evaluation session is to be meaningful, the manager must avoid dealing with the subordinate's performance. Instead, he must create an environment in which the employee understands that the supervisor's performance will be evaluated along with his own . . . The supervisor should learn from the employee how the supervisor can best serve his work-related needs while working on the project."[8]

During the interview, the employee should be encouraged to use this as a learning experience to make the decisions necessary for the coming year and to make the job performance as successful as can be. There needs to be a time for the employee as well as the employer to express concerns or to explain the situation from their point of view.

Interview

"Do not let any unwholesome talk come out of your mouths, but only what is helpful for building others up according to their needs, that it may benefit those who listen."
Ephesians 4:29 (NIV)

The interview is an integral part of the entire performance evaluation process. This is a time to engage in constructive dialogue, review the past, develop plans for the future, and provide encouragement.

Above all we must remember that we are dealing with people, and they should be treated with fairness, kindness and in a Christ-like manner.[9]

Give Adequate Notice

Employees should be given at least a week's notice of when the performance evaluation interview will take place. This will give them time to review their job description, any form(s) which will be used, and their goals and objectives.

Judy Block lists these steps to the interview process:

1. Set the tone at the start of the interview. Your aim is to relax your employees. Make clear that you are having a two-way conversation.

2. Ask the employee to evaluate his or her own performance.

3. Give your assessment of the employee's strong and weak points.

4. Summarize your own and your employee's views.

5. Develop an action plan in cooperation with your employee. Choose goals that are as specific and practical as possible. Focus on the two or three most important goals instead of all the areas that need improvement. Then, set up a timetable for reaching these goals and devise ways of measuring their achievement.

6. Conclude the interview. Summarize the main points once more. Emphasize the future actions the employee will take to improve performance, and schedule follow-up dates to review the progress. Try to conclude the interview on a positive note.[10]

Notes

[1] Myron Rush, *Management: A Biblical Approach*, Victor Books, Wheaton, IL, 1985, p. 197

[2] Robert G. Johnson, *The Appraisal Interview Guide*, AMACOM (A Division of American Management Association), New York, 1979, p. 3

[3] Robert B. Maddux, *Quality Interviewing: A Fifty Minute Series Book* (Revised Edition), Crisp Publications, Inc., Menlo Park, CA, 1988, pp. 6–7; 11

[4] Robert B. Maddux, *Effective Performance Appraisals* (Revised Edition), Crisp Publications, Inc., Menlo Park, CA, 1988, p. 27

[5] Maddux, p. 11

[6] S.E. Barnes, *The Personnel Manager's Handbook of Performance Evaluation Programs*, Bureau of Law and Business, 1985, p. 59

[7] S.E. Barnes, *The Appraisal Interview Guide*, p. 4

[8] Maddux, p. 11

[9] Charles A. Tidwell, *Church Administration Effective Leadership for Ministry*, Broadman Press, Nashville, 1985, p. 127

[10] Judy R. Block, *Performance Appraisal on the Job: Making it Work*, Executive Enterprises Publications Co., Inc., New York, 1981, p. 59–61

PAYING MORE ATTENTION TO AVERAGE ACHIEVERS

It's not hard to notice that some people are higher achievers than others. The situation makes supervisors wonder if time spent on the "average worker" is as valuable as time spent on the outstanding person. According to *Incentive* magazine, it is indeed worthwhile to work with those who are average.

The word itself holds a clue to why this is true. There are far more midrange people, so there is a far greater area where your effort can be productive. Further, their potential for improvement is greater.

Here are some of the ways *Incentive* suggests that average workers can be placed in situations where they will be more productive:

- **Team techniques**—By teaming excellent workers and some who are average, the stronger people often help those who need improvement.

- **Participative management**—Designing programs where people have a say in how work will be done can motivate all workers. In most cases, it isn't lack of talent that makes a worker just average. More often, it's lack of enthusiasm and desire, but when people contribute and are proud of it, enthusiasm will follow.

- **Positive reinforcement**—Rewards that come more frequently and at various stages of a program do more to maintain enthusiasm for your program. Give people a taste of winning, monthly or even weekly. Frequency of information is important. Instead of seeing a huge, distant goal, the average worker (and the outstanding person!) will see that reaching it is not so difficult when they see progress, even a little at a time.

- **Use training**—Gear the training for individuals toward reaching goals in your program.

- **Solicit feedback**—Find out what parts of the program people think are going well and what is making it more difficult.

- **Learn the likes and dislikes of your people**—Find out what kinds of mid-program incentives they like so you can offer motivating rewards even if they aren't costly.

While it's true that you can't bring a person from "average" to "ace" without revising poor work habits, these techniques can make revisions more welcome and more likely to be successful.

When people feel they are participating members of your team, you will find the average worker will be interested in how he or she can contribute even more to the team effort.

Chapter Nine

PERFORMANCE PROGRESS REPORTS EVALUATION FORMS

There are several types of forms being used in performance evaluation (some of which are known by different names for basically the same format), such as trait checklist, free form, responsibility rating, management by objectives (MBO), forced choice, critical incidents, graphic rating scales, behaviorally anchored rating scales (BARS), behavioral expectation scales (BES), essay, dimensionalized, and mixed standard scales. The three forms most common among the churches responding to my survey are graphic rating scale, essay and MBO.

Graphic Rating Scale

This is probably the most widely used performance evaluation method.[1] In graphic rating scales, qualities and characteristics of employee performance are listed and each trait is rated using a scale usually ranging from unsatisfactory to outstanding. In many cases narrative support for the ratings is shown, providing a basis for consistency among raters.

Graphic rating scales are fairly easy to develop and administer. The forms are standardized, permitting quantitative results and allowing comparability of individuals. The quantitative nature makes this form useful in allocating salary increases based on merit. This method may be best for technical positions where the measurement of performance against targets is impractical. A disadvantage is that the traits may not relate specifically to job performance and, therefore, may be susceptible to an inconsistency of standards of comparison among the various raters.[2]

Essay

The essay form contains little or no prescribed format for the rater to follow. The narrative of the rater contains a description of the employee's overall performance and his strengths and weaknesses. This format allows the supervisor to discuss job performance without being forced to discuss traits. This method is best when the evaluation is to be used for employee development. The essay form does not allow for comparison of individuals and is not well suited for salary administration.[3]

Management By Objectives (MBO)

Using MBO, the supervisor and employee agree to goals and objectives to be accomplished within a certain time. Periodic reviews are performed to determine if the objectives have been achieved or to review the progress toward the objectives.

Lee Iacocca instituted a quarterly review system for his executives at the Ford Motor Company. He would ask a few basic questions: "What are your objectives for the next ninety days? What are your plans, your priorities, your hopes? And how do you intend to go about achieving them?" Every three months each executive would meet with his subordinate to review the past accomplishments and chart the goals for the next term.[4]

MBO is an especially valid method for use with the ministerial staff.

Employee Progress Report

Employee progress reports are used by many businesses and institutions for good reason. Few tasks are more unpleasant than that of firing an employee. If a periodic record has been maintained covering the employee's problems and the employee has been systematically counseled, the task of firing is less burdensome.

Since the employee has seen previous progress reports—and has had warnings—he or she cannot feign ignorance of the problem or claim lack of a fair chance.

From a more positive standpoint, the use of written progress reports and counseling can save a borderline employee, and in some cases, produce a more effective worker.

Employee progress reports can also be used to document sustained superior performance and serve as the basis for special recognition and awards.

The following guidelines should be followed when using written employee progress reports:

1. The average employee is a satisfactory employee; consequently, most of your employees will be in the satisfactory group.

2. Do not be unduly affected by unusual or isolated incidents. (The appraisal should reflect the individual's "general standard" of performance.)

3. Rate objectively and on the basis of evidence. (The rater should eliminate personal prejudice as far as humanly possible.)

4. Rate in terms of accomplishments; try not to be influenced by what others say about the individual.

5. Avoid reference to "opinions" in evaluation discussions with the employee. Stay with facts.

6. General remarks, recommendations, and comments may be included on a separate sheet and attached to the form when applicable. Be sure the employee is aware of all factors before filing the report.

7. Employee progress reports should be treated as **sensitive records** and filed so as to be available only to the personnel supervisor.

Goals Always Precede Evaluations

"Evaluation calls us to measure performance against purpose. Good evaluation demands that standards of effectiveness or success should be established beforehand. Goals always precede evaluations."[5]

Performance Rating Definitions

Before you can properly conduct a performance review, you must know the meaning of the terms on the evaluation form or progress report. Following are definitions of one set of performance standards:

Exceeds Standards—Performance consistently surpasses standards for the job assignment. This category is to be used for truly outstanding performance.

Consistently Meets Standards—Performance consistently meets standards for job assignment and may exceed some standards. This category is to be used for strong performance.

Usually Meets Standards—Performance meets many but not all standards for job assignment. This category is to be used to identify areas for performance development.

Does Not Meet Standards—Performance does not meet standards of job assignment and is unsatisfactory.[6]

A variety of different forms are included in the last section of this resource.

Notes

[1] Wayne Cascio, "Types of Performance Measures" in *The Performance Appraisal Source Book*, Human Resource Development Press, Amherst, MA, p. 68

[2] John D. McMillan and Hoyt W. Doyel, "Performance Appraisal: Match the Tool to the Task" in *Performance Appraisal Sourcebook*, Human Resource Development Press, Amherst, MA, p. 46

[3] Ibid., p. 69

[4] Lee Iacocca, *Iacocca: An Autobiography*, Bantam Books, New York, 1984, p. 50

[5] Bruce P. Powers, *Church Administration Handbook*, Broadman, Nashville, 1985, p. 21

[6] "Performance Planning Workbook," Texaco, Inc. 1989

Four Goals
For Every Supervisor

It's obvious that getting people to do things is the primary job of a supervisor. But having them work as a team, doing what you want and when you want it done is the challenge.

Keep the challenge alive. It will take skill and imagination to keep interest high over the long run. Study your people. Move them to another position, or arrange for them to acquire new skills. There are people who aren't interested in learning new things, but others need to be continually challenged.

Be an ace motivator. Capture loyalty and build a team spirit by instilling your values. Be consistent in giving and following the rules of the game, and make sure everyone lives by your code. To be the best . . .

• Give them a mission to complete.

• Give them the tools to do it.

• Give them recognition for good performance.

Hire intelligently. If you have a say in who will work for you, approve only those you think will embrace your values. If new hires don't work out, find a way to get them out of your department.

Be committed to quality work, and have a way to measure results. Find out where your results are affected most, then take action that will keep the problem from arising again. This will create a climate for self-motivation.

Chapter Ten

IMPLEMENTATION OF PERFORMANCE APPRAISAL PLAN

By Simeon May, FCBA

When I first joined the staff of my church, I discovered the church was using an "Employee Performance Rating" form. To complete this brief form, the supervisor rated his subordinates on an overall performance basis by choosing either "outstanding," "consistently exceeds standards," "consistently meets standards," or "occasionally meets standards." There was no definition given for the term "standards." In addition, the form contained five lines for "remarks."

The form was used strictly for salary administration and not for employee development. The process was looked upon with disdain and deemed to be a time-waster. There was no staff support for the process.

When hard financial times hit the church, salaries were frozen. Since no raises were being issued, employee ratings were suspended. About this same time, some unhappiness began to build in the church toward certain staff members. I soon realized we were in desperate need of a formal method for staff development and appraisal for praise, discipline and constructive criticism.

I began my research into performance evaluations while the church was without a pastor. As I shared with some of the staff what I was doing, I received glaring looks and comments of "Why do we need that?" and "What for?" and "You're just going to make people mad." There was no way an evaluation process would be implemented without the support of a pastor.

Our new pastor joined the staff in April 1990. He explained to the executive staff that he planned to conduct quarterly reviews with us "a la Lee Iacocca" (see Chapter 9, page 1). I immediately sensed that I might have the pastoral support for a performance evaluation system and shared with him my plans. I received his whole-hearted support and encouragement.

Together we reviewed the many evaluation forms which I had collected through my survey. We decided to design a form which contained elements of the graphic rating scale, essay form and MBO. The pastor also desired for us to utilize a form that was no longer than one page, front and back, so that the process would not be perceived as cumbersome and arduous.

Our first draft of the form was shared with the other members of the executive staff for their comments. This group would be the primary ones completing the form. After making the recommended changes from the executive staff, the second draft was presented to the personnel committee for their approval. The final version of the form and the evaluation were then presented to the entire church staff.

Our plan included the conducting of formal evaluations semi-annually in March and October. The church's fiscal year runs from April through March. The October evaluations would be for employee development and behavior correction, while the March evaluations would also be used for determining merit pay increases.

The evaluation form and the process were explained to the staff more than three months prior to the first evaluation week in October. This gave the staff plenty of time to review job descriptions and gain a clear understanding as to what was expected of them.

Our first form included eleven trait statements on which an employee would be rated. The scale was a five level scale from zero to four with a narrative phrase describing each point on the scale. The eleven scores were then totaled and marked on a rating scale. For example, if a person scored all zeros, his performance was labeled "Unsatisfactory." If a person scored all ones or 11, his performance was labeled "Some Deficiencies Evident." If a person scored all twos or 22, his performance was labeled "Satisfactory." If a person scored all threes or 33, his performance was labeled "Exceptional." If a person scored all fours or 44, his performance was labeled "Clearly Outstanding." The form also included an essay section for the listing of strengths and weaknesses, and goals and objectives. There was a place for the employee to make comments, and spaces for the employee, the evaluator and the evaluator's supervisor to sign.

The first evaluation week went very well with only a few problems. One thing we tried to make clear from the beginning was that scoring a "2" meant the employee was doing what was expected and was performing satisfactorily. However, while we explained that a "2" meant "meets expectations," the wording on the form, in many cases, indicated that a "two" meant "average." The descriptive phrases on the form were revised for use in the March evaluation period.

We discovered that not all trait statements needed a five level scale. For instance, we decided that a person either looked acceptable for work or didn't, so we changed the Personal Appearance scale to a three-level scale. Some traits received a four-level scale. Finally, the description for scoring a "22" was changed from Satisfactory to Meets Expectations. The revised form garnered a much better reception.

The performance evaluation system is one which requires constant review and updating. In the future, I expect we will design separate forms for use with the ministerial and support staffs. We might eventually divide the support staff and have specific forms for the secretarial, food service and maintenance staffs. The executive staff may use more of an MBO process with the program staff.

Conclusion

The largest amount of time and energy will be spent implementing a performance appraisal system. However, once the evaluators and evaluatees become comfortable with the system, much less time and energy will be consumed. Bernardin says "It should be made clear to appraisers that performance appraisal is an important element of their jobs and that they themselves will be assessed on the extent to which they have effectively carried out this function. Perhaps this single factor, holding raters accountable for their ratings, just as they are held accountable for the administration of other expensive organizational resources, will do more to improve the effectiveness of a performance appraisal system than any other technique or intervention that could be recommended."[1] Already, our staff has discovered that the effort put into our system has been extremely valuable.

Notes

[1] H. John Bernardin in *Performance Assessment—Methods & Applications*, Ronald A. Berk (ed), The Johns Hopkins University Press, Baltimore, 1986, p. 302

Chapter Eleven

PERFORMANCE APPRAISALS FOR CHURCH EMPLOYEES?

By Al Cartwright, FCBA

"Cheer up," the pastor's wife said one night. "Things could be worse." So the pastor cheered up—and sure enough things got worse.

The pastor had been struggling with how he was going to handle a particularly worrisome church employee. It seems the employee's recent work efforts had deteriorated. Her productivity had declined over the past year, and her attitude had become poor. The pastor had tried during this period of time to help correct the employee's problem, but now it was obvious to the pastor that this employee had to go. That night he jotted a note to the personnel committee chairman to give the employee notice and terminate her.

Easy as that? Wrong. The committee chairman checked her personnel file and found that the pastor had been giving her excellent appraisals all along. The chairperson politely informed the pastor that her dismissal might not be such a good move. "With her attitude," the chairman said grimacing, "She's liable to go to court. You really don't want that."

It appears that this pastor had been taking the employee appraisal system too lightly. Many churches seem to blunder through these situations all too often. Church employees should be the best treated employees anywhere, yet secular employers usually do a much better job of treating their employees fairly.

A Morale Builder

An employee appraisal system is a good management tool. If it is properly conducted, an appraisal can help build morale, as well as improve performance and effectiveness. Does that sound too business-like? Churches big and small need to have people serving the Lord who can do an excellent job. Church congregations should expect productive staffs. There is a lot of work to be done, and it needs to be accomplished quickly, accurately and professionally.

Regretfully, there are many churches that do not have any kind of performance evaluations, or it is sporadic and ineffective. Your church needs to formalize an appraisal program. It should be a fair and systematic method of looking at an employee's performance.

Church employees should be the best treated employees anywhere.

What is a Performance Appraisal?

A performance appraisal or employee review is an organized, or systematic approach used to evaluate an employee's job performance. You should review:

- The employee's performance of his or her job requirements against set standards.

- The potential of this employee to assume more responsibility on the staff

- Deficiencies or shortcomings of the individual that need to be corrected

- Training, special or on-the-job, that will help the employee correct problem areas or develop professionally.

These performance reviews are helpful to the church for many practical reasons. The review may be an element of a merit system. It helps in making decisions regarding retention of employees at times of staff reduction. Employee appraisals help the pastor or personnel committees make decisions regarding promotions (or demotions, probations, training or bonuses).

Observation

It is a tough job to terminate or dismiss a church employee. Yet, from time to time you will hire employees who just don't quite cut the mustard. Sometimes your church will have a substandard employee who joined the staff by osmosis. First, this person was a volunteer who was asked to work as a part-timer. After serving for some time, this person was asked to come on full-time, although maybe not fully qualified for the position. In the event it does become necessary to let someone go, it is easier (not much) if you have a file that reflects the efforts to improve the employee's performance, but little or no improvement is shown.

What Are the Elements of an Effective Appraisal System?

There are many types of forms or checklists that help supervisors organize an employee review or appraisal. There are rating scales or multiple choices for evaluating job-related performance characteristics. Some are more of a narrative form of rating job performance. Some appraisals even rate employees compared to other staff members. Some methods will allow for setting goals and then measuring against reaching those goals.

I personally prefer an evaluation tool that will utilize several of the above methods. This tool might include a rating scale that identifies performance levels.

A rating scale that identifies performance levels:

1. **Exceeds Job Requirements**—This means the employee has sustained performance which totally exceeded full requirements of assigned responsibilities, leaving nothing to be desired.

2. **Meets Top Requirements of Job**—This means that sustained performance was considerably beyond full requirements of assigned responsibilities.

3. **Fully Meets Requirements of Job**—This means the employee's sustained performance resulted in the full and complete accomplishment of assigned responsibilities, considering length of employment, work experience and job knowledge.

4. **Meets Minimum Requirements of Job**—This means performance was generally satisfactory, but did not attain full and complete requirements of assigned responsibilities.

5. **Not Satisfactory**—This means the employee has not been able to accomplish the responsibilities of the position; has not met job requirements.

Position Accountabilities

A section that accommodates a list, in order of importance, of the performance objectives to be achieved during the rating period. It should include appropriate criteria for performance measurements. At the beginning of the rating period, the supervisor and employee should sit down and discuss and mutually agree on some goals and objectives for the rating period.

For Example—A position accountability I might submit to my pastor in one of my areas of responsibility, such as "personnel administration," would be 1) To work with the staff and pastor parish relations committee (personnel committee) to develop an effective, realistic staffing plan for this church's growing and dynamic ministries. Or in administration, 2) To work with staff, committees and church organizations to begin the development of comprehensive church operating guidelines. The goals and objectives do not necessarily have to have numerical goals. Some church staff members are turned off by the "numbers game." But, sometimes you may want to express magnitude to your goal such as, "Continue steps to develop a self-sustaining food service ministry that will feed 300 families at our midweek services."

The important thing is that the goals and objectives be mutually agreed to, so that you have a clear idea of what to strive toward. You may find in this meeting, that your supervisor may have some other priorities to add to your list.

Supporting Comments

A rating scale, such as the one shown above, should be used to show the level of performance for each of the position accountabilities listed. Supporting comments would be used to describe the results achieved for each of the performance objectives. Justify the rating by showing what the results were. This is important not only for the higher rating, but also to provide information on shortcomings when an employee is rated as meeting only the minimum standards or is not satisfactory.

Setting achievable goals and describing results and progress takes work by both the rater and the employee. It takes evaluation and then translating that to words that are positive, yet will provide criticism when necessary. The end result will be a better employee.

Performance Characteristics

Another section of the performance appraisal should include comments regarding the staff member's ability to meet standards relating to performance. The same rating scale can be used to describe an employee's performance level.

Performance characteristics can address job responsibilities that include work quality and quantity, work characteristics, and supervisory capability.

Work Quality and Quantity—These characteristics include, but are not limited to:

1. **Productivity**—Quantity of work and effective use of time. Does this employee promptly complete assignments to expected standards?

2. **Quality**—Accuracy, neatness and acceptability of work to expected standards.

3. **Work Organization**—Job knowledge possessed relative to position requirement. Uses initiative and judgment in organization of work.

> **The important thing is that the goals and objectives be mutually agreed to, so that you have a clear idea of what to strive toward.**

Work Characteristics—This evaluation area could include:

1. **Work Habits**—Adaptable and stable, yet creative in approach to job responsibilities, attendance and punctuality.

2. **Communications**—Communicates with supervisor and subordinates. Keeps fellow workers informed.

3. **Attitude**—Willingness and ability to work effectively with others. Friendly and courteous. Accepts supervision.

Supervisory Ability—If your employee has supervisory responsibilities, you may want to address these characteristics:

1. **Organization and Planning**—Organizes and plans group productivity. Establishes objectives and goals. Follows up. Prioritizes and manages time.

2. **Management Skills**—Leadership effectiveness. Delegates authority. Able to efficiently arrive at effective decisions.

3. **Supervisory Communications**—Communicates up and down. Skilled in handling employee grievances and counseling.

These are just a few characteristics that can be used to set the standards and identify an individual's ability to meet those standards.

Overall Evaluation

An overall evaluation of the staff member should be arrived at by considering the performance level achieved and position accountabilities accomplished. The last page of the Employee Review and Performance Appraisal is perhaps one of the most important. A remarks section should be provided to allow additional input or considerations to be made. There may be a place that the employee can describe his or her career plans.

Next, development needs should be discussed. Experience, assignments, education or personal improvements that would be helpful to the employee should be listed. Careful consideration must be made by the supervisor on a plan that would meet the development needs. This is an action plan that will help the employee improve his/her job performance. Special training, workshops and leadership seminars can be planned.

Suggestion

At budget preparation time, please include a line item that allocates money for continuing education or professional development for your staff, especially the support staff. In many churches those benefits are provided to the ministerial staff, but not the rest of the staff. Training will pay for itself in increased job knowledge and professionalism.

Finally, your appraisal form should have a place for the employee to describe their reaction to the evaluation and the development plan. Ask the employee to sign the appraisal.

Establish Procedures Or Guidelines

Write the procedures and follow up to insure that responsibilities are established, and appraisals are timely and fair. The reviewer of the appraisal should be the supervisor's supervisor. This will keep the reviewer abreast of the staff member's job performance and progress. Guidelines could include items below:

1. **Establish the rating period**—This time is normally once a year. Some churches require twice-a-year evaluations. This can be burdensome to a busy staff, but informal sessions can take place any time during the year to review progress towards one's goals.

2. **Your personnel committee and finance committee**—These committees need to aggressively pursue adopting a staff merit program for your church. At budget time they need to determine a percentage of salary pool for staff merit increases.

3. **Usually the personnel committee** (or comparable organization in your church) will review the appraisal and makes the final determination of the recommended merit percentage increase. Their final decision on the merit percentage will be based upon the aggregate merit pool and the employee's rated performance. The personnel committee should have the prerogative to interview employees and/or supervisors where clarification is required.

4. **The committee** will then return the performance appraisal to the supervisor. The supervisor would then present the appraisal to the employee. Notification of a merit increase may have to wait until the ministry budget is approved by the church.

5. **The employee** will sign the appraisal when he/she has been apprised of his/her performance and evaluation. The signature does not imply agreement or disagreement, but merely acknowledges receipt. The employee should have the right to address any questions or disagreements to the personnel committee at a mutually acceptable time.

6. **The committee chairperson, church treasurer, or church administrator** (if you have one), after receiving the signed Employee Evaluation Form would then authorize the financial secretary or bookkeeper to enter the new salary rate into the payroll data at the appropriate time.

Caution

Problems can develop when implementing an appraisal system if the evaluations are not uniformly administered. The pastor needs to monitor the program and train where necessary. One thing to avoid is to arbitrarily give inflated or deflated appraisals across the board. Outstanding appraisals as well as unsatisfactory ones should be supported by sufficient rationale.

Conclusion

An employee review and performance appraisal system is effective and beneficial to any church if it is a well-planned process and administered fairly to all employees. The written appraisals can provide the basis for taking personnel actions. Good procedures will also protect the church. Church employees must be treated fairly. There have been more incidents recently where disgruntled employees have tried to involve attorneys and sometimes go to court because they feel they have been treated unfairly.

Why a Performance Appraisal?

As supervisors we sometimes make daily snap judgments about the secretary who works for us. We may not even think about it consciously. "She always seems to mess up the telephone messages," or "That newsletter looks good, but it seems to need more graphics." Judging on a day-to-day basis would be OK, I guess, but would not get us down the road to achieving desired goals.

We really need to take the time to sit down and establish a plan for development of our staff. We should establish standards and then measure our employees against them. We should think about the experiences, assignments, education and personal improvements that our employees need to achieve those goals. The appraisal is so very important in making judgments about what kind of training or improvement is needed for our staff team to reach its maximum potential. We owe it to them and the Lord.

Al Cartwright, FCBA, a former business administrator, lives in Indian Rocks, Florida.

Chapter Twelve

MINISTERIAL STAFF: TO EVALUATE OR NOT TO EVALUATE?

"Performance reviews for pastors are basically nonexistent."

"Many pastors see as a role model the evaluation Jesus received of his ministry by the Pharisees and the Roman governing authorities—they crucified him!"

"No one is qualified to evaluate the pastor."

"A performance review can be a delicate and risky event in the pastor-board relationship."

"We simply cannot appraise spiritual matters. How can we appraise spiritual attitude?"

These and other similar statements are found in many articles about performance evaluations regarding church staff members, particularly the pastoral staff.

A significant obstacle to evaluating the pastor is the difficulty of developing an effective evaluation procedure. Other obstacles have to do with wondering "Is it worth the effort?" and the reluctance of clergy to subject themselves to a potentially excruciating experience.[1]

Other writers note the risks but contend that pastors are being evaluated in some way, and it is better to have some control over the evaluation process and have it be a constructive experience.

Martin Thielen, writing in the *Church Administration* magazine, asks, "How does a pastor get feedback on his ministerial performance?…Tying professional identity and performance to numbers alone is inadequate." Although not recommended by others, Thielen suggests one method of evaluation is receiving feedback through an anonymous pastoral evaluation. This would be done perhaps during Bible study time with all adults and youth participating. The key in this type of evaluation is to look for trends and not to be too concerned over isolated, negative comments or criticisms. For the most part this is an affirming experience.[2]

In an article in *The Christian Ministry* magazine, Lyle E. Schaller points out, "Smaller churches tend to evaluate their minister in personal rather than professional terms…The larger churches tend to think in functional terms and therefore are more likely to attract a task-oriented pastor." The congregation of a smaller church might praise their pastor with the following statements:

- "Our minister loves everyone!"

- "From almost the very first day she called everyone by name, and she remembers the other people in your family!"

- "He's such a wonderful family man. He has a wonderful wife and three lovely children."

- "He really knows how to get out and meet people; the last pastor sat in his study in the manse most of the day."

The focus shifts when this question is asked in churches averaging between 100 and 200 in Sunday morning worship. Those affirming their pastor tend to extol individual leadership characteristics:

- "He's a great organizer."

- "Our new pastor is one of the most creative people I've ever known."

- "Our new minister is the best preacher we've had in years."

In the larger churches, and especially in those with multiple staff members, the comments suggest a different role. In those congregations the commendations often emphasize the role of the pastor as the leader of an organization.

- "He's really got this church moving. For years we seemed to be drifting aimlessly. Now we act like we have a purpose."

- "He has built an excellent staff, and they work together in a way I never believed possible."

- "She's got everyone working together."[3]

In the *Church Administration* magazine, Jerry Poteet states, "I have been encouraged to involve our staff in performance appraisals partly because I realize that we are being appraised whether we have a system or not. All church staffs are appraised either formally or informally; either by a system designed to gain an accurate appraisal of staff performance or by a collection of opinions, speculations, or innuendoes." He lists four things that are important in developing an appraisal system for a church staff.

1. The process of development should begin with the staff and not with the personnel committee or any other committee or group in the church. The church staff should be totally involved in every phase of the development of the system. Staff members feel threatened and even defensive when a personnel committee devises the system of appraisal and then announces to the pastor and staff that it is about to be implemented. It is equally unwise for the pastor and personnel committee to develop a system without the involvement of the other staff members.

2. Invite a knowledgeable professional to train the staff in the fundamentals of position descriptions and performance appraisals.

3. Develop an appraisal document that will meet the needs of your staff. It is helpful to look at many appraisal documents before writing your own. The staff and personnel committee should work together in developing this appraisal docu-

ment. It should be specific enough to cover all areas of work performed by the staff members, yet general enough to apply to all members of the staff.

4. The appraisal system should allow staff members to be appraised by more than one or two phases. The system we finally settled on, provides four phases of appraisal for each staff member. These include an appraisal based on the Standards of Performance, the Interest Group Appraisal, the Supervisor's Appraisal, and the final review performed by the personnel committee. (See also information about standards on page 29.)

Rev. Poteet answers "yes" to the following five questions in his article.

1. Is it possible to develop an effective appraisal system for church staffs?

2. Is it wise to develop an appraisal system for church staffs?

3. Should an appraisal system include evaluations of all staff members from pastor down to part-time custodian?

4. Should the results of an appraisal system affect monetary compensations of the staff?

5. Should the laymen of the congregation have a significant part in the appraisal process?

It is not only possible but prudent to develop an effective and comprehensive appraisal system for church staffs.[4]

Larry Osborne, writing in *Leadership* magazine, gives some steps for creating a process that's positive, not poisonous.

Initiate the Process

Initiating the process offers several benefits. It disarms most potential enemies. An evaluation I've requested is radically different from one imposed by others. Once critics realize I actually want to hear what they have to say, they will often become less intense—less likely to feel they have to shout or overstate their case for me to hear them.

It allows a measure of control over the participants. Call the process a personal evaluation rather than a job performance review.

It allows a measure of control over the process.

I overcome the biggest obstacle to personal growth: my defensiveness. . . .When I ask for a critique, instead of feeling attacked, I feel assisted. Instead of playing the role of an employee worried that the bosses might not be happy, I'm a leader soliciting candid advice. The difference is significant.

Choose the right time

Avoid intense reviews during times of great stress or when struggling with feelings of failure.

Don't take anonymous feedback

Anonymous feedback undermines an effective review and fosters misunderstanding. By its nature, an anonymous response makes clarification and explanation impossible.

Get it in writing

Written appraisals avoid many pitfalls, encourage input from all, and can't be altered by the consensus of the meeting.

Change evaluation tools

After using the same evaluation tool for two years in a row, I discovered that what prompted helpful analysis the first year, produced short, superficial answers the second. Changing the evaluation tool gets feedback in many areas.

Keep salary separate

Distinguish between a pastoral review and a salary review.

Faithful Wounds

The controlled environment of a pastoral review keeps one from being unfairly criticized by antagonists. Instead, I had received the faithful wounds of friends. And there is no comparison between the two.[5]

Haak and Speilman conclude their article, "Who Should Evaluate The Pastor," by stating, "We would underscore that the presence and use of a regular evaluation procedure is a sign of a healthy and growing pastor. Formal evaluation provides opportunity for personal renewal and reflection. It should not be an intrusive procedure, but a personal matter to assist church professionals in their functioning in whatever role they are fulfilling. It is an important component of professional growth and development."[6]

As you can see from the above information, there are a variety of ideas about evaluations for the pastoral staff. It is something that takes much thought and careful planning. Most agree that evaluation is taking place, whether in a positive, productive manner, or through criticism whispered in the hallways and parking lot, depends on guidance given by the leadership.

Richard F. Gordon answers the question "Does your performance appraisal system really work?" The following is a summary of portions of his article.

Barriers To Assessing Performance

Poor design of most performance-assessment programs is one barrier.

Wrong performance criteria places the employee in a position of being evaluated against standards over which he or she had no control.

Vague performance criteria which does not specify the desirable employee behavior. If an employee does not know, or fails to understand the importance of the job standards, the performance assessment program will not serve its intended purpose.

Many supervisors simply fail to weigh performance factors objectively. They tend to rate each factor or scale according to their overall impression of the employee rather than make an independent judgment for each factor.

Some of the variables which affect evaluation are:

- Prejudices and biases of assessors

- Attitudes of management and employees toward performance assessment

- Lack of training in how to assess performance

- Guidelines for objective performance evaluation

Key Components

It requires commitment to have an effective performance evaluation system. Some of the key components of an objective performance evaluation system are:

Attitude. A positive attitude can be contagious.

Job Standards must be realistic, achievable, and under the control of the employee. Should specify what constitutes good, average or marginal performance. Must be communicated to the employees, preferably in writing, prior to the start of the evaluation time period. Established standards must be adhered to by supervisors when they evaluate an employee.

Timeliness reflects the supervisor's attitude toward the system and the priority being placed on the program. Systematic scheduling allows the supervisor time to think more carefully about the employee's performance and thus avoid snap judgments.

Feedback may be the most beneficial aspect of the evaluation process. It affords the supervisor an opportunity to reinforce the behavioral changes accomplished during the rating period. Should be clear and specific and directed towards behavior that the employee can do something about.[7]

Notes

[1] Harold H. Haak and Larry W. Speilman, "Who Should Evaluate The Pastor," *The Clergy Journal*, February, 1994, pp. 45–46

[2] Martin Thielen, "Receiving Feedback From Your Congregation," *Church Administration*, Nashville, October 1998, p. 17

[3] Lyle E. Schaller, "Evaluating The Minister: What Does Your Pastor Do Best?", *The Christian Ministry*, March 1984, pp. 12–14

[4] Jerry M. Poteet, "Church Staff Performance Reviews/Appraisals," *Church Administration*, Nashville, July 1981, pp. 14–16

[5] Larry Osborne, "How To Get A Healthy Performance Review," *Leadership*, Spring 1994, pp. 118–120

[6] Hoak, pp. 45–46

[7] Richard F. Gordon, "Does Your Performance Appraisal System Really Work?", *Supervisory Management*, February 1985, pp. 37–41

ITEMS FOR PERFORMANCE EVALUATION/APPRAISAL

1. How well does the staff member enlist, develop and supervise staff members, laity and seminary interns?

2. How well does the staff member carry out what has been planned?

3. Has the staff member followed through with professional development plans—that is movement on a career path?

4. How well has the staff member integrated his/her program area with the other program areas of the church?

5. How well has the staff member lived within the parameters of the church budget?

6. How has the staff member's plan been carried out—that is have plans been adjusted to meet changing circumstances? . . . has staff member been able to maintain program momentum during the year? If not, why?

7. What is the feedback from the staff member's supervisor and lay leadership with whom they work?

8. What are the statistical gauges that show growth?

9. What has been the overall involvement in working with new members and/or prospects and visitors?

10. What are the priorities that the staff member has placed on the fulfillment of his/her job description for the coming year? Has the staff member demonstrated those priorities in planning and results?

11. How much time away has the staff member had? What was the time used for? Does it help the staff member fulfill personal and work-related development plans? Does it help the church move toward accomplishing its stated ministry?

Chapter Thirteen

NEW EMPLOYEE ORIENTATION

By Edward R. Lycett, FCBA

Most people have some memory of their first day on the job. For some it is pleasant, for others, it is one they might choose to forget. "A good program of employee induction—helping the new worker get a good start—should provide a thorough introduction to the overall work of the church and the staff so that (he) may understand the framework in which he operates."[1] The church ought to be an environment where individuals feel welcome and secure. Many churches spend a lot of time and money in orienting new Christians and church members and training teachers to accomplish their tasks. Many times in the church environment we just hand a new employee a job description and a green light to begin work. Some do not receive as much as a job description. Then we wonder why the performance is not what we thought it would be during the employment process.

Setting some goals and objectives before an employee starts can, in the long run, be an aid to effective performance later. "Objectives give us a sense of direction and purpose. They define what we want to accomplish and provide a way to measure our success. Objectives are a road map that take us from where we are to where we want to be. An effective new employee orientation program will accomplish the following objectives. It will:

1. Provide a genuine welcome.

2. Develop positive perceptions about the organization.

3. Confirm the employee's decision to join the organization.

4. Teach basic fundamentals each new employee should know.

5. Provide a basis for training.

6. Put the employee at ease."[2]

Most new employees arrive at work the first day full of enthusiasm and excitement. If we have **A New Employee Orientation Program**, we can build on this excitement and nurture it for the future. New employee orientation is not difficult and need not consume a large amount of time. In fact, when done properly, orientation will save time in the long run. The goal of orientation is to capitalize on each new employee's enthusiasm and keep it alive once the work begins. When orientation is successful, a new employee will become a valued asset to the organization.[3]

New worker orientation begins with the interview process that is initiated before employment is offered. "When a job is discussed with the applicant, the following items, at a minimum, should be covered.

• Background of the organization

• General job description

• Performance evaluation procedures

• Work hours

• Compensation

• Vacation and time off

• Benefits

• Probation period"[4]

Some employers prepare a packet of information that is given during the employment interview stage. Different types of information could be included in this packet, such as the following.

- Name, address, and phone number of organization

- Names and titles of key staff and committee chairpersons

- A brief history of the organization

- Normal working hours and pay periods

- Vacation and time off policies

- Medical and other benefits

- Type of new hiree probation period

- Contact person following the interview

- Specific job description(s)

If this information is not included in a prospective employee packet, then it should be provided during the orientation program.

Hopefully during the interview process, we have made enough of an impression with the prospective employee to make them want to serve as a part of our organization, realizing it is more than a job, it is a ministry. "Once a job has been accepted and a starting date has been agreed upon, the first thing to do is clear your schedule. Orientation is not a time to be out of town or locked up in meetings.

As a supervisor, you are responsible for getting things started during the orientation. It is not the responsibility of a secretary or another employee to do your job. They may be involved, but the new employee should not be assigned to anyone until you have made the initial contact and established a plan for the day."[5]

Some things that need to be taken care of during orientation:

- Make sure an employee application is filled out and on file.

- Paperwork for payroll, health benefits, etc.

- Make I.D. card or key to gain access to the building if necessary.

- A tour of the work place should be given.

- Introductions to co-workers should be made.

- Equipment that will be used should be supplied and/or explained.

- Employee handbook should be provided and any explanations needed about terms of employment should be handled.

Orientation is a procedure that will take more than one day. It may be a process that lasts throughout a probationary period. The orientation period should be a time to help employees become all that they need to be.

Notes

[1] Leonard E. Wedel, *Church Staff Administration: Practical Approaches*, Broadman Press, Nashville, p. 32

[2] Charles M. Cadwell, *New Employee Orientation*, Crisp Publications, Los Altos, CA, 1988, p. 1

[3] Ibid., p. 3

[4] Ibid., p. 25

[5] Ibid., p. 34

Chapter Fourteen

TEAM BUILDING

By Edward R. Lycett, FCBA

From the beginning of time, individuals and groups have been dealing with the concept of team building whether it was called that or not, trying to establish a home, develop community or learn to work with each other. This is probably the most misunderstood concept in the area of staff relations. Most people believe just because they are on a church staff or part of a business relationship they are a team. Most would accept the following definition, taken out of context, to be that of a team . . . "A team helps people accomplish more than they could working individually."[1]

The best definition I have found has been developed by the American Management Association. "The most distinguishing characteristic of a team is that its members have, as their highest priority, the accomplishment of team goals. They may have strong personalities, possess highly developed specialized skills, and commit themselves to a variety of personal objectives they hope to achieve through their activity, but to them, the most important business at hand is the success of the group in reaching the goal that its members, collectively and with one voice, have set. The members support one another, collaborate freely, and communicate openly and clearly with one another.

Most "non-team" groups, on the other hand, tend to be collections of personalities with their own agendas, which may be more valuable to those personalities than the agenda that the majority of the group members seek to fulfill. Discussions and relationships in such groups are often characterized by shifting agendas, power subgroups, a "going along" with decisions rather than a wholehearted commitment, and even a win-lose orientation: One person or subgroup gains its wishes over another."[2]

As I read this definition, cold chills ran over me. Through my experiences, I have realized the difference between church staff "teams" and other types of "non-team" or church groups. Being an attender for a number of years at staff events, it is not hard to realize that one of the largest problems we have in our churches is that of the "staff dis-ease," or staff members being unhappy where they are and with those with whom they serve, "...a person really doesn't have to be psychotic, neurotic, incompetent, inexperienced, or even unspiritual to encounter this problem."[3]

Being able to be a team member, "results in benefits for both team members and the organizations in which they work.[4] They are:

- Collaboration

- Communication

- Application of resources, talents and strengths

- Decisions and solutions

Collaboration, the primary benefit, results because people want to work together. They have a desire for the team to be successful, and individual competitiveness is reduced. For the sake of what it will produce, they want to do more than cooperate with one another.

Communication is another benefit. Individuals who have respect and have learned to trust and support one another pass information back and forth so the team will operate better. Because of this, there is a more efficient application of resources, talents and strengths. This happens because the team members are willing to share what they have with other members of the team.

The fourth benefit is **decisions and solutions** which are made simultaneously because everyone is able to generate and evaluate more than one person can develop.

Robert E. Bingham has described this lack of "team" evident on many church staffs as *"ecclesiastical arteriosclerosis."* Some of the symptoms of this malady within staffs are:

- Broken or clogged lines of communication

- Unresolved conflict between staff members

- A lack of respect for one another's calling, training, skills and work

- Insufficient planning, coordination and cooperation

- Broken trust in relationships

- Power struggles with the staff

- Imbalance between responsibility for work and the authority to do the work

- Critical attitudes, rationalization, perfectionism, self-depreciation and competitiveness

- Lack of close, supportive relationships

- Unresolved feelings over differences in salary scales

If a leader chooses not to place a high value on teamwork, it will not occur. Teamwork takes consistent effort for it to be developed and continuous effort is needed for maintenance to occur. The rewards can be great. It is the choice of the leader.

Notes

[1] Myron Rush, *Management: A Biblical Approach*, Victor Books, 1990, p. 48

[2] Thomas L. Quick, *Successful Team Building*, American Management Association, AMACON Work Smart Series, New York, 1992, p. 3

[3] Jerry W. Brown, *Church Staff Teams That Win*, Convention Press, Nashville, 1979, p. 7

[4] Quick, p. 13

Chapter Fifteen
A PROCESS FOR FORMULATING A PERSONNEL MANUAL

By Dr. W. Maynard Pittendreigh, Jr.

Each congregation is different, but in general, the following steps can be used as a guideline for any congregation to follow.

Step One—Review the current staff policies. There might not be any that are written, but there are some that are inferred by tradition or other unwritten manner.

Step Two—Review the current staff. Who works at the church? What are their titles? Do they have job descriptions? What do they really do? How do the staff members interact? Among these findings, what needs to be retained and what needs to be changed or modified?

Step Three—Review the current legal issues involving employment. This is in a constant state of change. What is current at this point may not be current when you are ready to do your study.

Step Four—Review the current denominational policies regarding staffing. The Presbyterians have their Book of Order. Congregationally-governed churches might not have such a denominational system of rules.

Step Five—Compile a list of questions the personnel manual needs to address. This list ought to include the following:

1. What are the categories for an employee?

2. How are staff reviews conducted? When and by whom?

3. What policies will there be regarding personnel files?

4. Will employees be required to be church members, or will there be a policy in which church members will not be employed?

5. What is the policy regarding giving out references? Will there be a neutral policy? Who will give references?

6. Will there be a statement regarding sexual or other harassment in the work place?

7. What are the different staff positions? A job description will be needed for each.

8. What are the prerequisites for each job?

9. Will there be a probationary period for new employees?

10. How will hiring take place?

11. How will termination take place?

12. What is the disciplinary process?

13. What leave provisions will be established for holidays, vacations, study leave, sick leave, paternity or maternity leave, and emergency leave?

14. What policies will there be regarding salary administration? When is payday? When are raises given?

15. Will there be a dress code?

16. Will there be a faith statement all must subscribe to?

17. How will the personnel manual be introduced to present staff?

18. How will the personnel manual be introduced to future staff, and how and by whom is orientation conducted?

19. Who will review this manual, and at what frequency?

Step Six—Write the manual. A manual such as this might best be done as the work of one individual, who then takes it to committees for review and revision. At some point, I suggest that the present staff be engaged in this process of review and revision. Doing this brings in their unique skills of creativity and insight, and helps reduce their own anxiety about being given a personnel manual full of rules for them to follow.

Step Seven—Approve the manual. Have the governing body of the church officially approve the manual. In a Presbyterian congregation, this is the Session.

Step Eight—Have the manual printed.

Step Nine—Introduce the manual to the staff. Sufficient time should be given to introducing this to staff members.

Step Ten—Use the manual. It will be the tendency for the governing body or the staff to forget it, but use it and keep it alive and visible.

Recognizing that all churches are different, having moved through this process, I believe these are the minimum basic questions that must be asked in putting together a personnel manual for any congregation.

Chapter Sixteen

COACHING YOUR TEAM TOWARD SELF-MOTIVATION AND TEAM GOALS

By Joyce Parchman

As a supervisor your work in motivating people gets faster and more direct results than big programs designed to do the job. You can't be there looking over the shoulder of each person on your team, so your goal is to make people want to work well. You must create a climate of self-motivation and still maintain a team spirit. The team must work as a unit; each one self-motivated, while working as a team toward a common goal.

A Good Image and Personal Satisfaction

To achieve a climate of self-motivation, help your team create a good image and set standards for personal satisfaction.

The newscaster on TV has an image that is carefully built, so does the president. Public relations experts build images for "important people," but you and I don't have that service. We have to create our own.

Who needs it? Does pumpkin pie need whipped cream? Does cheesecake need strawberries? Without them, these desserts wouldn't be ordered as often in restaurants. Creating a good image is one step in creating a climate for self-motivation.

Professionalism

Lead your team to be professional, whether they work mowing the yard, cleaning the buildings or running a computer. Help them to understand the importance of their job and how to do it well. Be sure they know what they are supposed to do and when—know what they have agreed to do. Then check to see if they know for certain how to do the job. Sometimes that isn't clear. When they ask questions, get the information they need. Be a coach.

Tell them what you expect all along the way, but be open for feedback.

Growth

Allow them to upgrade their skills. Being professional about work also means knowing there is always more to learn. Encourage your people to grow. Sign them up for training and education classes. Include them in idea-generating talks about how to do the job in more effective ways. Insist they read whatever is available about the equipment they use and the work they do.

Courtesy

Be courteous. It's a mirror of your character and your team's character. Show your appreciation regularly for specific jobs done well. Your courtesy will spread to your team members.

Productivity

Expect them to deliver. Business consultant Paul Stern says "to deliver means to do the tasks that have been set in front of you better than anyone else in your position is expected to."

Identify barriers to productivity. Ask each employee what stands in the way of his or her being more productive. Ask what you do that gets in the way of productivity. (You could get some eye-openers on this one.) Remember that doing consistent good work is important.

Philip Van Auken in his book *The Well-Managed Ministry* (Victor Press, 1989) noted that in secular organizations, "Achieving results ordinarily takes precedence over how results are accomplished." He continues, "Christian organizations must not define efficiency only in this narrow economic sense. Christian goals should not be achieved at the expense of people."

Hard Work

Demonstrate the meaning of "hard work"—it involves creating excellence. Hard work is physical or mental labor that is measured not only in hours but in output and quality of results. Get reinforcement from those around you. As a part of a productive team, you work better and enjoy the acceptance of others on the job.

Two-way Communication

Encourage communication. Provide opportunities for each member to talk about his or her job. Stay in contact with your team and handle problems as they arise. Better yet, handle them before they become problems. Make sure communication is two-way so ideas flow freely.

Involvement

Get your team involved in the quality improvement process. All of us have been asked to become involved in making decisions about various aspects of our work. We must take this issue seriously.

The American Society for Quality Control agrees. A Gallup poll commissioned by the society shows that when employees are asked to rank several ways to better work performance, the number one answer chosen was: "Letting you do more to put your ideas into action." The survey also came up with one fact that was disturbing. Quite a few employees responding to the poll felt there was a gap in what their companies said was important and how the company responded to their suggestions on reaching those goals. Not every idea can be acted upon immediately, but keep your team thinking. Personal involvement in the quality improvement process is part of a self-motivation climate.

Team members must be fully aware of the mission of the church. Van Auken says, "By 'catching the strategic vision,' ministry members will be more motivated and stronger team members."

Coaching

The climate for self-motivation is a little like the weather. It changes every day. The good supervisor must be sensitive to changes in how individuals feel about their work and keep those feelings on the positive side. Dr. Ken Blanchard states:

A good performance management system consists of three parts: performance planning, which involves setting goals; day-to-day coaching, to help staff members accomplish their goals; and performance evaluation, to examine each individual's performance against goals during a certain period. . . . The step that is almost never done well is day-to-day coaching.

Coaching should take up 90 percent of your people management efforts. It enables you to help your staff monitor their progress and systematically move toward success.

A review of 24 studies on job turnover published in *Academy of Management Journal* shows that good performers are significantly less likely to leave a company than underachievers.

For managers, this means that time taken to help a poor performer become better will have a double effect. The poor performer becomes a good worker and will be less likely to leave the organization.
As you build your team, think from day to day about what makes your people feel good about themselves and take pride in their work. Your coaching can bring enthusiasm and response that exceed expectations.

Coaching includes intervening quickly when workers become unproductive, and developing the strongest team members to become leaders and mentors to others on the team. It includes cheerleading from the sidelines when team members are under stress and underachieving. A good coach places each team member in the correct niche for optimum performance and is willing to make sacrifices for his team as well as lead them to sacrifice for one another—thus building a strong network of support. This type of spirit empowers the team to work together for a common goal—accomplishing the ministry of the church.

The image you and your team display is valuable. It lets others know what kind of people you are. Team members should be professional in their work, try to learn more about it, and make excellence a priority. Like strawberries on the cake, a good image, personal satisfaction and self-motivation will make your team stand out and reflect Christ and the mission of your church.

Joyce Parchman is former Director of Publications for NACBA.

Chapter Seventeen

A DIFFERENT LOOK AT PERFORMANCE REVIEWS
DEVELOPMENT REVIEW

By Gary F. Smith

A recent newspaper article from the Knight-Tribune News Service began as follows, "The employee performance evaluation may be one of the most hated rituals in the modern American work place." Yet for years performance reviews have been an integral part of an organization's staff management discipline. Churches on a broad scale have also incorporated the performance review in the management of their staffs.

Of course, everyone's ultimate performance review is found in 1 Corinthians 3:13 (TEV):

"And the quality of each person's work will be seen when the Day of Christ exposes it. For on that Day fire will reveal everyone's work; the fire will test it and show its real quality."

Although Christ's review will test our work for Him according to our spiritual calling, employees may often feel *tried by fire* when they are on the receiving end of performance reviews for their earthly work as well.

This article will describe the characteristics of most performance reviews in use today, some of the drawbacks to this management tool, and suggest an alternative for use in the church working environment.

Traditional Performance Reviews

The traditional rationale for an organization's use of performance reviews is to create an historical record of employee productivity and effectiveness and to highlight problem areas and/or training and development needs. They are typically given annually, either at an employee's anniversary (hire) date or at year-end, are often tied to a salary increase and

usually involve a meeting between supervisor and employee.

To facilitate the review, various forms have been developed listing several of the following employee attributes which the supervisor is asked to evaluate using some type of rating scale:

- Job knowledge and skills

- Quantity and quality of work

- Flexibility and adaptability

- Initiative and creativity

- Attendance and punctuality

- Appearance and dress

- Interaction with others

- Attitude and teamwork

In addition, the review form often contains provisions for establishing and measuring staff objectives, developing training programs, and/or an overall rating of the employee's performance during the period covered by the review.

Once the form is completed, the supervisor typically meets with the employee to discuss the ratings and objectives, suggest corrective action where necessary and, in some cases, warn the staff member of the consequences should perceived performance deficiencies not be corrected in a timely manner. Employees are usually asked to sign the review to indicate they have read the document and are often given the opportunity to write their own comments on the review form. The review is then placed in the employee's permanent file.

Drawbacks To The Traditional Review

Virtually since inception, the review process described previously has been subject to various criticisms, the most serious of which are the following:

1. Performance reviews are often the source of employee/supervisor tension; staff members can become defensive or even hostile during the interview, leading to arguments and ill will. This is particularly true if problem areas are not addressed as they occur, but are accumulated and then *dumped* on the employee during the review.

2. Reviews are subject to rater errors and bias; supervisors often tend to rate those in highly paid jobs higher, give more weight to recent events, rate with a *halo* effect, and can let personal bias creep into the review. They may also give artificially high ratings to avoid confrontation.

3. Reviews tend to be more subjective than objective; often the employee's behavior and personality traits are given more weight than her/his knowledge or skill level.

4. Employees are often preoccupied with the rating, especially when a salary change is involved. Staff frequently view or focus on the rating as a *grade* (A-E), and can miss entirely the constructive parts of the review intended to enhance their growth and development.

5. Reviews, typically conducted only annually, can take the place of frequent employee/manager communication and feedback. Often used in place of timely disciplinary action, employees can view the whole process as basically punitive in nature.

More recently, management experts such as the late W. Edwards Demming, a pioneer in the development of Total Quality Management (TQM) systems in Japan and the United States, have proposed that most of the factors which affect staff performance and productivity are beyond the employee's control and that an individual employee's contribution can-not be fairly or accurately measured. Further, asserted Demming, time spent assessing individual staff performance within a work system could be better spent improving the system itself.

An Alternative

These concerns about the traditional performance review process have caused many organizations to question whether employee contributions can be fairly and accurately measured *and* whether the value of doing so outweighs the potential negative impact on staff motivation, cooperation, and self-esteem.

Approximately two years ago, the administration committee of First Presbyterian Church of Flint, Michigan, determined that the potential negative impact of the traditional performance rating process warranted a change in both the philosophy and conduct of staff reviews. In its place, the church committee created an alternative process which emphasizes staff growth and development activities but eliminates performance ratings and subjective judgments regarding employee behavior or personality traits. Titled simply the *Development Review*, the revised procedure focuses on staff strengths and personal objectives to enhance both their individual skills and their ministry areas.

The Development Review Has Four Major Sections

Section I: Skill Development—In this opening section, the supervisor is asked to comment on the staff member's knowledge, skills or other factors relevant to her/his current growth and development. This part of the review is open-ended; however supervisors are instructed to refrain from subjective comments regarding behavioral or personality traits.

Section II: Completed Objectives—Personal employee objectives established during the previous review and completed during the review period are described here, as well as appropriate comments regarding results.

Section III: New/Continuing Objectives—In this space, comments are made relative to previous objectives still in process. In addition, any new and mutually agreed-upon objectives and actions necessary for their completion are described in this section.

Section IV: Personal Training Plan—This last part provides the opportunity for reviewer and employee to develop a training *menu* for the coming review period with target dates for completion. The training plan should enhance those skills identified in Section I and/or help the employee achieve the objectives described in Sections II and III.

The review concludes with notations of approval by the employee, the ministry head and/or the senior pastor, with the opportunity afforded the employee to add any additional comments to the form as they wish.

The Development Review is conducted at least annually in mid-year, while salary reviews are performed at year-end, thus providing maximum separation of the two events in the minds of the staff. However, supervisors and staff are free to use the review at any time they feel it to be appropriate.

In use for two years at First Presbyterian Church, the Development Review has been received very favorably by staff and evaluators alike. The tension and anxiety which at one time accompanied the annual performance review process has been replaced with a time of constructive suggestions and feedback, conducted at more frequent intervals, and all pointed toward the goal of improving the quality of church ministry.

What about File Documentation?

Eliminating the traditional, ratings-based performance review may cause some initial concern among those who feel it is essential to file employee documentation. Without *regular*, objective evaluations, argue its proponents, disciplinary actions against an employee would become difficult in an environment where the courts are playing an increasing role in employee-employer relationships.

In reality, however, few traditional performance reviews are useful for such documentation purposes because of the subjectivity, and the tendency for

supervisors to avoid confrontation. At the other extreme, relying *solely* on a performance review for employee disciplinary purposes reinforces its image as a feared, punitive technique which staff can strongly resent, and which may even foster future problems with the employee.

Employees who experience problems on the job should be counseled daily, weekly or as often as necessary. Documentation regarding these specific issues should be placed in the file immediately. Relying on a once-a-year performance review to *lower the boom* on an employee almost certainly creates a *lose-lose* situation for both staff and the organization.

Summary

When the Development Review was in its design phase at First Presbyterian Church, a member of the administration committee observed that the development of the church staff was a Christ-like activity to which considerable energies should be devoted. Equipping and upholding our employees to serve our congregation and community in a manner pleasing to God is a top priority in our church. The Development Review has become an important tool to help us achieve that end.

Gary F. Smith is the business administrator at First Presbyterian Church, Flint, Mich.

Chapter Eighteen
CONSIDERATIONS FOR A PERFORMANCE REVIEW PLAN

I. Definition

A performance review can be defined as a team meeting scheduled to review commonly agreed upon goals: discuss the employee's contribution; explore necessary work performance adjustments; agree upon short and long range goals, actions and support; and to communicate salary.

II. Objectives

1. Validate selection process

2. Identify high potential employees

3. Measure performance with goals

4. Employee development

5. Administration of rewards

III. Value Of Employee Appraisal

1. Motivational—recognition for work performed, challenging goals set which will give the employee an opportunity to achieve, building a strong relationship based on mutual confidence, and providing opportunity to give praise, strokes, and recognition.

2. Administrative—provide objective data for salary decisions, promotion, transfer, terminations, etc.

3. Informative—discussion of mutual expectations, past performance and goal achievement, recognition of an individual's needs and value system, feedback on supervisory style.

4. Developmental—identification of strengths and weaknesses, development goals and strategies determined, help employees improve their performance.

IV. Assumptions: People Work Better When They Know:

1. What they are supposed to do.

2. What authority they have.

3. What their relationships with other people are.

4. What the performance standards are.

5. What they are doing exceptionally well.

6. What their major weaknesses are.

7. That there are equitable rewards for good work.

8. That what they are doing is of value.

9. That the supervisor has an interest in and concern for them.

10. That the supervisor wants to have the employee succeed and progress.

V. Outcomes

1. Improved performance and productivity

2. Development of the employee

3. Feedback to the manager and employee

4. An objective performance evaluation tied to salary increases

5. High potential candidates identified

6. Answers to these recurring questions:

   a. What should the individual's reward be?

   b. Where does the individual best fit in the organization?

   c. How can the individual be helped to perform better?

   d. How well are organization programs working?

VI. Tools For Performance Appraisal (All Written And Dated)

1. Job description

2. Performance standards (objective statements)

3. Goals (measurable and dated)

4. Incident file (feedback file—letters, reports, events, actions)

VII. Advantages of a Standardized Goal/ Results-Oriented Performance Appraisal Plan

1. Greater employee commitment when employee is involved in determining his own goals and standards, and therefore his own performance yardstick.

2. Provides an objective review with less chance of disagreement when the goals are properly determined (attainable, challenging, within the employee's authority) and stated (clear, specific, measurable)

3. Lets the manager and employee know of the progress on goal achievement.

4. Provides identification with the organization's goals and mission.

5. Motivates employees by:

   a. giving them recognition for work accomplished,

   b. participation in setting challenging goals,

   c. providing an opportunity for achievement.

6. A standard performance appraisal plan helps to insure fairness and equity throughout the organization.

7. It provides objective data for performance evaluation and salary allocation.

8. Places an emphasis on results, not process. This would also enhance employee creativity.

9. It helps managers to be better day-to-day supervisors.

10. It aids manager/employee communication.

11. It is future oriented

VIII. Limitations of a Goal/ Results-Oriented Performance Appraisal Plan

1. Learning to set good goals and standards is difficult.

2. Goals must be attainable yet challenging.

3. Mutual goal setting may be illusory—the supervisor actually setting them and not negotiating the goals with the employee.

4. May over-emphasize the measurable.

5. May blur individual responsibility—if you have joint goals, the responsibility could be shifted.

IX. The Appraisal Interview Process

1. Preparation

   a. Schedule the review and communicate it several days prior to the review.

   b. Develop a format.

   c. Evaluate your own performance in relationship to the employee.

   d. Continually build an atmosphere or climate which encourages the exchange of ideas and feeling about the job.

   e. Complete the appraisal and have confidence in it before you start the interview.

   f. Provide suitable physical arrangements for:

      i. Privacy

      ii. Physical comfort

      iii. Near or in the employee's work area

      iv. Time allocated

   g. Collect the objective data for the review. Categories of data are:

      i. Feedback data

      ii. Coaching data

      iii. Promotion/merit data

      iv. Long-term data

   h. Document your appraisal by use of goal achievement, performance standards, development records, incident file and previous review.

   i. Preparation checklist

      i. How will the employee react? How will you handle the reaction?

      ii. Can you support the performance rating with objective facts and incidences?

      iii. What are the employee's strengths which you will comment on?

      iv. What major weaknesses are you prepared to discuss?

      v. What corrective action(s) do you want the employee to take?

      vi. Have you developed a training plan for improving the employee's skills?

      vii. Which of the employee's personal traits do you want employee to develop?

      viii. How will you help the employee do this?

      ix. In what way will this performance rating affect the employee's chances for a promotion?

2. The Interview

   a. Open the interview by telling the employee the general purpose of the interview.

   b. If the employee has performed good work, give the performance rating at the beginning. If the work has been unsatisfactory, avoid definite statements at the beginning, but reveal it gradually by self-examination or a series of individual appraisal statements.

c. Tailor your approvals to the individual under consideration. You should consider:

   i. Personal traits, interests, reactions and value system.

   ii. The type of work being done.

   iii. Does employee want to improve her performance.

d. Make the appraisal interview compatible with your day-to-day relationship with the employee.

e. Make a smooth transition from one area to another.

f. Create a climate in which the employee is free to express himself.

g. Link the interview with the employee's future.

h. Be an active listener.

i. Areas to discuss include:

   i. Strengths for which you have supporting data.

   ii. Major weaknesses for which you have supporting data.

   iii. Goal achievement and corresponding performance level.

   iv. Development plans.

   v. Suggestions for the supervisor as to her management style.

   vi. Negotiate new goals and performance standards.

   vii. Merit/structure raise.

3. Concluding the interview

a. Conclude the interview when the employee:

   i. Has an accurate idea of mutual expectations and present performance.

   ii. Knows what improvement is expected.

   iii. Knows what plan of action will help achieve the desired improvement.

   iv. Has agreed upon goals and performance standards.

b. Restate the major conclusions and plans.

c. Provide a transition back to the normal workday atmosphere.

d. End the interview on a positive note.

4. Follow-up

a. Hold to your side of any commitments.

b. Provide ways for the employee's development.

c. Provide period reviews (without merit) for goal achievement.

d. Use the feedback you received on your management style.

X. The Appraisal Development Relationship

1. Identifying of strengths and weaknesses

2. Providing constructive feedback

3. Developing a plan for development

a. Establish outcomes

b. Establish action plans

c. Establish time frames

4. Discussing career aspirations

5. Questions employees ask themselves

XI. Review Unsatisfactory Performance

1. Suggestions for coping with the situations

2. Benefits from constructive confrontations

XII. Common Errors Made In Appraisal

1. Lack of preparation

2. Not allowing enough time

3. Not setting a climate for "sharing"

4. Operating off of biases

5. Over-emphasizing a single incident

6. Making generalizations from specifics without adequate support

7. Assuming if an employee can do one task well that is all he can do

8. Emphasizing activities rather than results

9. Letting personal likes/dislikes have an influence

XIII. How to Improve the Appraisal of Employees

1. Reduce the time interval between appraisals

2. Evaluate on consistent performance and not on what has been done "recently"

3. Provide feedback, positive and negative, in a constructive developmental manner

4. Reinforce strengths

5. Identify deficiencies and establish developmental plans

6. Clarify job expectations

7. Discuss career aspirations

8. Schedule the interview, allowing enough time for supervisor and subordinate to prepare

9. Allow sufficient time for the review

10. Follow-up

11. Recognize the "new-generation" employee

12. An understanding of management's responsibility for employees performance

Don McCain 1985

EVALUATE YOURSELF

What type of a manager are you? Use the matrix below to evaluate yourself. Have your best friend and someone who works closely with you (an associate or secretary) fill out the matrix and compare it with yours. It might be very revealing as you examine your management style and see how others perceive you.

Item		Degree		Number
Boldness, audacity	Risk taking	1 - 2 - 3 - 4 - 5	Cautious	_____
Pressure, pace	Relaxed	1 - 2 - 3 - 4 - 5	Rigorous	_____
Personal relationships	Supportive	1 - 2 - 3 - 4 - 5	Demanding	_____
Decision-making speed	Fast, quick	1 - 2 - 3 - 4 - 5	Studied, worried	_____
Decision-making approach	Authoritative	1 - 2 - 3 - 4 - 5	Consultative	_____
Type of follow-up	Loose, little	1 - 2 - 3 - 4 - 5	Much, rigorous	_____
Openness to persuasion	Flexible	1 - 2 - 3 - 4 - 5	Stubborn	_____
Work with superior	Wants support	1 - 2 - 3 - 4 - 5	Works alone	_____
Availability	Easily available	1 - 2 - 3 - 4 - 5	Remote	_____
Analytical patterns	Intuitive	1 - 2 - 3 - 4 - 5	Analytical	_____
Communication	Informal, verbal	1 - 2 - 3 - 4 - 5	Formal, written	_____
Explicit rules of thumb	Few	1 - 2 - 3 - 4 - 5	Many	_____
Delegation	Little	1 - 2 - 3 - 4 - 5	Much	_____
Work with subordinates	One-on-one	1 - 2 - 3 - 4 - 5	In a group	_____

THE EMPLOYEE PERFORMANCE REVIEW

I. Setting Performance Goals

1. Review job description
2. Review annual plans
3. Consider special projects
4. Identify expected key results
5. Participatively establish goals with standards that specify: What is to be done, when, how much, how many, how well, with what resources
6. Goals should be: Significant, challenging, specific, measurable, understandable, attainable, results oriented, job related
7. Identify criteria for current performance level and next performance level

II. Preparing For Performance Review

1. Schedule review in advance
2. Provide for privacy, comfort, communication
3. Ask employee to complete forms, bring to review
4. Review data from reports, accomplishments, feedback
5. Complete forms
6. Analyze review to ensure:
   Fairness, consistency, equity, legality, objectivity, explainability

III. Conducting Performance Review

1. State purpose of review
2. Establish communication climate
3. Review employee's completed forms
4. Discuss goals achieved, affirming praiseworthy performance
5. Review performance on additional assignments completed
6. Assess performance on goals not achieved; explore problems
7. Recognize potential and strengths, citing examples
8. Identify and provide written documentation for performance problems
9. Explore career aspirations
10. Decide upon development plans
11. Elicit feedback on supervisory style
12. Restate main points of review
13. Secure signatures, indicating discussion has taken place and date
14. Communicate salary decision
15. Set and clarify goals and standards for next review period

APPENDICES

EMPLOYEE PERFORMANCE EVALUATION FORM

Name _____ Evaluation Date _____

Ministry/Department _____ Job Title _____

Please circle the number to the left of the descriptive phrase which most nearly describes the person being evaluated.

A. Accuracy is the correctness of work duties performed.

0 Makes frequent errors.	1 Careless; makes recurrent errors.	2 Usually accurate; meets expectations.	3 Requires little supervision; is exact and precise most of the time.	4 Requires absolute minimum of supervision; is almost always accurate.

B. Alertness is the ability to grasp instructions, to meet changing conditions and to solve novel or problem situations.

0 Slow to "catch on."	1 Requires more than average instructions and explanations.	2 Ability to grasp instructions meets expectations.	3 Usually quick to understand and learn.	4 Exceptionally keen and alert.

C. Creativity is talent for having new ideas, for finding new and better ways of doing things and for being imaginative.

0 Rarely has a new idea; is unimaginative.	1 Occasionally comes up with a new idea.	2 Imagination meets expectations; has reasonable number of new ideas.	3 Frequently suggests new ways of doing things: is very imaginative.	4 Continually seeks new and better ways of doing things; is extremely imaginative.

D. Dependability is the ability to do required jobs well with a minimum of supervision.

0 Requires close supervision; is unreliable.	1 Sometimes requires prompting.	2 Takes care of necessary tasks and completes with expected promptness.	3 Requires little supervision; is reliable.	4 Requires absolute minimum of supervision.

E. Job Knowledge is the information concerning work duties which an individual should know for a satisfactory job performance.

0 Needs constant follow-up on routine procedures & assignments.	1 Lacks knowledge of some phases of work. Requires follow-up on routine assignments.	2 Has know-how & skills to meet job assignment. Requires instruction & follow-up in unusual & new circumstances.	3 Understands all phases of work. Requires very little follow-up.	4 Has complete mastery of all phases of job.

F. Quantity of Work is the amount of work an individual does in a work day.

0 Does not meet minimum requirements.	1 Does just enough to get by.	2 Volume of work satisfies job requirements.	3 Very industrious; does more than is required.	4 Superior work production record.

G. Stability is the ability to withstand pressure and to remain calm in crisis or stressful situations.

0 Goes "to pieces" under pressure; is "jumpy" and nervous.	1 Occasionally "blows up" under pressure; easily irritated.	2 Has expected tolerance for crises; usually remains calm.	3 Tolerates most pressure; adjusts to crises better than the average person.	4 Thrives under pressure; really enjoys solving crises.

H. Courtesy is the polite attention an individual gives other people.

0 Blunt; discourteous; antagonistic.	1 Sometimes tactless.	2 Always polite and willing to help.	3 Inspiring to others in being courteous and very pleasant.

I. Personal Appearance is the personal impression an individual makes on others. (Consider cleanliness, grooming, neatness and appropriateness of dress on the job. Consider the nature of the job.)

0 Very untidy; poor taste in dress.	1 Sometimes untidy and careless about personal appearance.	2 Satisfactory personal appearance.

J. **Attendance** is faithfulness in coming to work daily and conforming to work hours.

0 Often absent without good excuse and/or frequently reports for work late.	1 Lax in attendance and/or reporting for work on time or leaves work occasionally.	2 Usually present and on time; stays expected hours.	3 Always regular and prompt; volunteers for overtime when needed.

K. **Budget Control** is the ability to work with and within the church approved budget.

0 Shows no concern for budget.	1 Occasionally fails to stay within budget.	2 Almost always stays within budget.	3 Exemplary in working with budget.

Summary Score

Total all of the numbers circled ☐ and mark on the rating scale.

0	11	22	32	39
Unsatisfactory	Some Deficiencies Evident	Meets Expectations	Exceptional	Clearly Outstanding

Major areas needing inprovement:

1. _____

2. _____

3. _____

These can be strenghtened by doing the following:

_____

_____

_____

_____

Major strong points are:

1. _____

2. _____

3. _____

These can be used more effectively by doing the following:

_____

_____

_____

_____

_____   _____
(Signature of Evaluator)   (Signature of Evaluator's Supervisor)

Employee Comments

You, the employee being evaluated, should use this section to make any comments you feel appropriate regarding this evaluation or points applicable to your supervisor.

_____

_____

_____

A copy of this Evaluation Form has been shared and discussed with me.

_____   _____
(Employee's Signature)   (Date)

EMPLOYEE PERFORMANCE EVALUATION

Name _____ Job Title _____

Date of Employment _____ Department _____

Appraisal Date _____ Appraisal Period _____

Part I - To Be Completed For All Employees

General Characteristics

Communication with Supervisor	Fails to inform supervisor of progress or problems ( )	Occasionally neglects to inform supervisor of work status ( )	Generally keeps supervisor informed of progress or problem ( )	Superior at keeping supervisor informed ( )	Exceptionally adept at communicating with supervisor ( )
Attitude	Attitude negative or indifferent ( )	Casual, sometimes lacks interest ( )	Job commitment is good ( )	Attitude reflects interest and concern ( )	Presents good work image excellent attitude ( )
Stability	Unable to work under pressure or in crisis situation ( )	Occasionally shows effect of pressure or conflict ( )	Maintains calm under pressure or conflicts ( )	Tolerates more pressure or conflict than average ( )	Complete control in problem situation ( )
Courtesy and Cooperation	Often Uncooperative; discourteous ( )	Sometimes blunt, discourteous, uncooperative ( )	Normally courteous and cooperative ( )	Polite, tactful, willing to cooperate ( )	Agreeable pleasant to a commendable degree ( )
Adaptability	Inflexible Resists Change ( )	Difficult to change ( )	Moderately adaptable ( )	Very adaptable adjusts quickly ( )	Exceptionally versatile ( )
Attendance and punctuality	Often Absent without good excuse and/or frequently reports for work late ( )	Lax in attendance and/or reporting for work on time ( )	Regular in attendance; usually punctual ( )	Very regular in attendance; very prompt ( )	Always regular and prompt ( )
Personal Appearance	Often Untidy or inappropriately dressed ( )	Sometimes untidy and careless ( )	Usually well groomed and neat ( )	Careful about appearance ( )	Always appropriately and neatly dressed ( )
Acceptance of supervision	Negative or indifferent toward instructions/supervision ( )	Sometimes seems resentful toward instruction/supervision ( )	Follows instructions and accepts supervision ( )	Positive acceptance of instructions/supervision ( )	Welcomes instruction/supervision as means of professional growth ( )

Work Characteristics

Job Knowledge	Poorly informed Constantly requires assistance ( )	Lacks knowledge of some phases of work. Often requires assistance ( )	Adequately informed for job ( )	Good knowledge understands all phases of work ( )	Thorough comprehensive knowledge and mastery ( )
Judgment	Judgment cannot be relied on ( )	Judgment often faulty ( )	Judgment usually sound ( )	Judgment consistently sound ( )	Judgment well above average ( )
Personal Efficiency	Frequent inefficient use of time ( )	Does not always use time efficiently ( )	Satisfactory utilization of time ( )	Very efficient rarely wastes time ( )	Highest degree of efficiency ( )
Problem Recognition	Does Not recognize until too late ( )	Occasionally fails to recognize ( )	Usually anticipates before they occur ( )	Superior in problem recognition ( )	Always perceives problems before ( )
Organization of Work	Unable to manage workload priorities; inconsistent ( )	Often allows workload to build up; has difficulty prioritizing ( )	Handles workload with normal ability Good prioritization ( )	Very good at organizing priorities and managing workload ( )	Exceptionally adept at managing workload & setting priority ( )
Initiative	Always awaits instructions; indifferent ( )	Relies heavily on others. Often needs reminding ( )	Works independently ( )	Industrious; willing to do more ( )	Exceptionally diligent ( )
Creativity	Rarely has a new idea ( )	Occasionally comes up with a new idea ( )	Has average imagination; reasonable number of new ideas ( )	Frequently suggests new ways of doing things; very imaginative ( )	Continually seeks new & better ways of doing things; Extremely imaginative ( )
Budget Control	Shows no concern for a budget ( )	Occasionally fails to stay within budget ( )	Usually stays within budget ( )	Almost always stays within budget ( )	Exemplary in working with budget ( )
Follows Church Policies & Procedures	Shows little regard of church policies & procedures ( )	Occasionally follows policies and procedures ( )	Generally follows church policies and procedures ( )	Almost always observes church policies and procedures ( )	Always observes policies & procedures ( )
Overall Evaluation	Inadequate ( )	Below requirements ( )	Meets requirements ( )	Exceeds requirements ( )	Outstanding ( )

B-1

List specific items that document the employee's completion of his job description and performance standards.

List recommendations for improvement.

List action steps that will help the employee improve his job performance.

List training activities that you recommend the employee utilize to improve his job performance.

Part III - To Be Completed Only For Employees Who Hold Supervisory Positions

Supervisory Ability					
Leadership	Unable to lead effectively ( )	Shows little leadership ( )	Displays average amount of leadership ( )	Leads well ( )	Excellent leadership abilities ( )
Supervisory Decision Making	Ineffectual decision making ( )	Faulty judgment; requires supervision ( )	Decisions consistent with facts ( )	Sound decisions promptly made ( )	Highly effective decision making ( )
Delegation of Authority	Extremist (too little or too much) ( )	Has problem with appropriate delegation ( )	Normally effective ( )	Delegates wisely ( )	Extremely skillful delegator ( )
Supervisory Organization And Planning	Disorganized Weak in planning ( )	Has problems organizing and prioritizing ( )	Consistent priorities; satisfactory planning & organizing ( )	Well planned and organized ( )	Thoroughly planned and organized ( )
Group Productivity	Well Below established goals ( )	Somewhat below established goals ( )	Meets Established goals ( )	Exceeds established goals ( )	Outstanding productivity ( )
Supervisory Communication	Weak in training or informing staff ( )	Occasionally inadequate performance ( )	Average communication skills ( )	Frequently superior performance ( )	Highest degree of skill ( )
Employee Management	Poor handling of employees grievances counseling & discipline ( )	Fair handling of employee grievances, counseling & discipline ( )	Average handling of employee grievances, counseling & discipline ( )	Good handling of employee grievances, counseling & discipline ( )	Superior handling of employee grievances, counseling & discipline ( )
Overall Evaluation ( )	Inadequate ( )	Below requirements ( )	Meets requirements ( )	Exceeds Requirements ( )	Outstanding ( )

Part IV - General Remarks by Supervisor, Give Brief Narrative of Evaluation Interview With Employee

Part V - (Optional) General Remarks By Employee. Comment In This Section If You Do Not Concur with The Evaluation.

Part VI - Overall Job Performance Evaluation. (Check One) - Note: Rating Does Not Represent An Average Of The Ratings, But An Indication Of The Employee's Total Job Performance.

☐ 1. Employee is an outstanding performer in all phases. Performance exceeds requirements in all aspects of the job.

☐ 2. Employee is an above average performer. Performance exceeds requirements in many areas of the job.

☐ 3. Employee is a satisfactory performer. Performance meets job requirements.

☐ 4. Employee is a marginal performer. Employee requires improvement in one or more areas of work to meet job requirements.

☐ 5. Employee is an unsatisfactory performer. Employee is to be informed and improvement in performance must be demonstrated within 30 days.

Employee's Signature: I hereby certify that this rating has been discussed with me by my supervisor.   Title   Date

( ) I Concur   ( ) I Do Not Concur

Supervisor's Signature   Title   Date

Signature of Reviewer   Title   Date

Approved By Personnel Committee   Chairman   Date

B-3

EMPLOYEE'S SELF REVIEW

This questionnaire will help you prepare for discussion with your supervisor. These questions are intended to help you think objectively about your job, your assignments, your capabilities in handling these assignments, and your future. Do not feel limited in your discussion to the questions listed. On the other hand, don't feel that an item must be covered if it seems inappropriate.

1. Review your job description and performance standards. In what tasks have you excelled?

2. What tasks need improvement?

3. Are there changes you would like to see made in your job content or organization of your work group which would help you to be more efficient?

4. What skills do you have that could be used more effectively by the association? Are there parts of your job where more information or training would help you improve your performance? (If so, please explain)

5. What factors do you feel may have affected your performance during this rating period?

6. What steps have you taken to increase your abilities and prepare for the future?

7. What additional items would you like to discuss?

Signed _____ Date _____

CORRECTION ACTION RECORD

Instructions: Supervisor is to complete this report in duplicate. Keep original in employee's department file and forward duplicate to master Personnel File.

Name _____ Job Title _____

Date of Occurrence _____

Action Involved   ☐ Verbal Warning   Has verbal warning been given?   ☐ Yes   ☐ No
                         ☐ Corrective Interview

Facts Involved

_____

_____

_____

_____

_____

_____

_____

                           Supervisor's Signature   Date

Employee Comment Portion (Not applicable for verbal warning)

_____

_____

_____

_____

_____

_____

I have read the above statement and understand that it constitutes a warning. I understand, too, that continuation of this infraction of church rules or policy will result in my dismissal.

                           Employee's signature   Date

A signature does not necessarily indicate agreement.

Action Taken

_____

_____

_____

_____

B-5

THIRTY DAY PERFORMANCE REVIEW
For New Employee Date of Review

Employee's Name	Job Title	Supervisor's Name	Date of Hire

		Check One		
		Satisfactory	*Unsatisfactory	Not Observed
People skills	Cooperation with co-workers			
	Attitude			
	Responds cooperatively to supervision			
Learning of job skills/knowledge	Ability to learn job functions & responsibilities			
	Demonstration of what is learned			
Dependability	Attendance			
	Punctuality			
	Follows through on instructions			
Activity level	Initiative			
	Effort expenditure			
	Ability to keep pace with work flow			
Overall Performance Evaluation				
Job Description	Review Job Description & performance standards with new employee. Document any items as needed below.			

Document each area rated "Unsatisfactory" with specific job-related examples in space provided below
Attach additional sheet if necessary.

_____   _____
Employment Recommendation   Supervisor's Signature   Date

☐ Retain ☐ Terminate

B-6

PERIODIC PERFORMANCE REVIEW

Plans for Improvement and Development. (This form will be completed by both the Supervisor and the employee during the Periodic Performance Review.) Briefly state the improvement or developmental goal(s) and list the action steps you have agreed upon to accomplish the goals.

Improvement or Developmental Goal(s):_____

_____

_____

_____

Action Steps: _____

_____

_____

_____

Training: What training activities would you recommend the employee utilize to help accomplish goal(s)?
Name(s) of Activities _____

_____

_____

Recommended date for completion of training: _____

Employee will know she/he has accomplished the goal(s) when: (state in <u>observable</u> and measurable terms.)

_____

_____

_____

Supervisor will review progress made on the Action Plan on: (date)_____

Employee Comments: (After the discussion the employee uses this space to record any reactions.)

_____

_____

Employee's Signature*	Date	Supervisor's Signature	Date

* This signature indicates that the employee has seen the Performance Review and that a discussion has taken place with his/her supervisor. (Signature does not necessarily indicate agreement.)

** Copy of Plans for Improvement and Development to employee and supervisor.

** Completed Periodic Performance Review form filed in employee's Personnel File & Master Personnel File.

Evaluation of Supervisor

Rate on Scale 1 to 5
(Leave blank if unobserved)

_____ Ability to plan workload

_____ Handles disagreements appropriately

_____ Treats employees with respect

_____ Willingness to assign work

_____ Willingness to do supervisor's own work

_____ Interest in worker's problems

_____ Willing to take responsibility

_____ Willing to take on extra work

_____ Knowledge of job

_____ Ability to respond to difficult situations

_____ Overall supervisory ability

_____ Promptness

_____ Ability to accept criticism

_____ Ability to finish job

_____ Willing to talk about problem areas

_____ Ability to do supervisor's job

Employee Performance Evaluation

Employee's Name: _____ Title: _____

Date Employed: _____ Date Mid-Year Review: _____

Length of time supervisor has managed employee's performance: _____

Reviewed by: _____ Title: _____

Approved By: _____ Title: _____

DEFINITION OF LEVELS:

1. MARGINAL — Does not meet desired standards in a number of important responsibilities and overall performance is considered unsatisfactory. Plans to improve or possible removal from job.

2. BELOW EXPECTED — Meets the standards of the job generally, but in the performance of some responsibilities has not yet met desired standards. Performance is considered somewhat marginal.

3. SATISFACTORY — Generates the desired results; may excel at favored work assignments. Performance is considered as generally satisfactory. Accomplished what the job was designed to do.

4. OUTSTANDING — Performance consistently generates results above those expected of the position or results in extraordinary and exceptional accomplishments. Contributes in a superior manner to innovations, technical or functional. Employee remains flexible and can salvage situations. (It is anticipated that very few will attain this level of excellence.)

SUPERVISOR'S EVALUATION

Employee's Name:_____

Mid-Year Date:_____

Final Date: _____

Staff Member's Performance Objectives	* EMYR	+ SMYR	# EFR	" SFR

* EMYR = Employee's mid-year rating
+ SMYR = Supervisor's mid-year rating
# EFR = Employee's final rating
" SFR = Supervisor's final rating

D-2

EMPLOYEE'S PERSONAL EVALUATION

Employee's Name:_____

Date: _____

AREAS OF RESPONSIBILITY	STAFF MEMBER'S PERFORMANCE LEVELS											* EMYR	+ SMYR	# EFR	" SFR
	Outstanding		Above Expected		Satisfactory		Below Expected		Marginal					
	+	-	+	-	+	-	+	-	+	-				
Attainment against expected performance														
Attitude														
Ability to work with others														
Dedication to the church and the job														
Ability to follow up projects														
Ability to listen														
Utilization of time														
Desire and necessary preparation for Advancement														
Support of total church ministry														

* EMYR = Employee's mid-year rating
+ SMYR = Supervisor's mid-year rating
# EFR = Employee's final rating
" SFR = Supervisor's final rating

EMPLOYEE'S PERSONAL EVALUATION

EMPLOYEE'S NAME _____

DATE _____

EMPLOYEE'S
SELF EVALUATION OF PERFORMANCE

STRENGTHS:

_____
_____
_____
_____
_____

GROWTH AREAS:

_____
_____
_____
_____

ACTION STEPS:

_____
_____
_____
_____

COMMENTS:

_____
_____
_____
_____

D-4

EMPLOYEE PERSONAL EVALUATION

EMPLOYEE'S NAME: _____

DATE: _____

Personal job satisfaction:

1	2	3	4	5	6	7	8	9	10
Low				Average				High	

Overall effectiveness rating

1	2	3	4	5	6	7	8	9	10
Low				Average				High	

Comments: _____

_____

_____

_____

_____

_____

_____

_____

_____

_____

_____

_____

_____

REPORT OF PERFORMANCE

_____ First (6 Months)
_____ Second (1 Year)
_____ **Yearly (Date of employment _____)**

NAME (Last First Initial)	SOCIAL SECURITY NUMBER	DATE OF REPORT
JOB TITLE	DEPARTMENT	

QUALIFICATION FACTORS	RATINGS ARE INDICATED BY "X" MARK		
	IMPROVEMENT NEEDED	GOOD	OUTSTANDING
1. CHRISTIAN GRACES - observable testimony including, but not limited to, language, countenance, kindness, mercy, patience, joy, self-control, gentleness, personal witnessing and service.			
2. EMOTIONAL CONTROL - capacity to work under the strain of spiritual warfare.			
3. SKILL - expertness in doing specific tasks; accuracy; precision; completeness; neatness; quantity.			
4. KNOWLEDGE - extent of knowledge of methods, materials, tools, equipment, technical expressions and other fundamental object matter.			
5. WORK HABITS - organization of work; care of equipment; punctuality and dependability; industry; follows good practices of vehicle and personal safety.			
6. RELATIONSHIPS WITH PEOPLE - ability to get along with others; effectiveness in dealing with the public, other employees.			
7. LEARNING ABILITY - speed and thoroughness in learning procedures, policies and other details; alertness; perseverance.			
8. ATTITUDE - enthusiasm for the work; willingness to conform to job requirements and to accept suggestions for work improvement, adaptability.			
9. ABILITY AS SUPERVISOR - proficiency in training employees and planning, organizing, assigning and getting out work; leadership; understanding of and effectiveness in implementing departmental and church personnel management policies.			
10. ADMINISTRATIVE ABILITY - promptness of action; soundness of decision; application of good management practices; understanding and effective implementation of departmental and church management policies.			
OVER-ALL RATING (the over-all rating must be consistent with the factor ratings and comments, but there is no prescribed formula for computing the over-all rating.)			

COMMENTS TO EMPLOYEE (supervisor should include factual examples on work done where improvement is needed. It is helpful if examples of outstanding work are also cited. Over-all ratings of "improvement needed" or "outstanding" must be substantiated. Use additional sheets if more space is needed.)

Immediate Supervisor _____Date _____ Department Head _____ Date _____
I HAVE REVIEWED THIS REPORT WITH MY SUPERVISOR. Signature of employee _____ Date _____

COPIES: Original to Personnel File; Copy to employee; Copy for departmental use

E-1

Job Performance Evaluation

I. GUIDELINES

1. A problem with an employee should be dealt with immediately instead of waiting until the formal review time.

2. Employees operating at the below satisfactory level in more than two areas should be given a plan to improve and notified of possible dismissal if improvement is not achieved.

3. Reviews should be conducted at mid-year and end of year.
    (December/January and July/August suggested)

4. Employees who are supervised by more than one person should be rated by all supervisors and supervisors decide who will conduct formal interview. All evaluations to be shared with employee.

II. RATING SYSTEM (Question 9)

The rating will be scaled for effectiveness in each of the seven categories.

1. Rate in each category as follows:

Rating	Rate Range (rate by .5 increments)
Below Satisfactory	0-4
Satisfactory	5-6
Surpasses Satisfactory	7-8
Far Exceeds Satisfactory	9-10

2. Place rating in far right column.

3. Add all ratings and place total at bottom of right column.

4. Divide total by seven to arrive at overall average which becomes basis of merit employee would receive. The range and percent of merit are as follows:

Rating	% Merit	Rating	% Merit
0-4.5	0	7.5	75
5.0	50	8.0	80
5.5	55	8.5	85
6.0	60	9.0	90
6.5	65	9.5	95
7.0	70	10.0	100

PERFORMANCE EVALUATION
Secretarial-Clerical Maintenance

Instruction: Supervisor complete in triplicate.
Keep original and give duplicate to employee.
Both copies brought to scheduled meeting.
Triplicate copy to next upward level of supervision.

Employee	Job Title	Date
Completed by Supervisor		

1. Based on this person's job description and your observation of the work produced by this employee which skills listed below are engaged in. Please circle.

Receptionist	Shorthand	Editing	Custodial
Typing	Transcription	Layout	Machine repair
Computer operations	Grammar	Art Work	Painting
Filing	Spelling	PBX	Furniture repair
Human Relations	Punctuation	Communications	Carpentry
Other (name)	Other (name)	Other (name)	Equipment operator
			Other (name)

2. In which skills checked do you feel this employee excels?

3. In which skills checked do you feel this employee needs to improve?

4. What improvement plans, if any, were agreed upon in the performance review?

F-2

JOB PERFORMANCE EVALUATION
Secretarial-Clerical Maintenance

Instruction: Employee completes in duplicate.
Keep original for use in scheduled meeting.
Give duplicate to supervisor at the meeting.

Employee	Job Title	Date
Completed by Employee		

1. Based on your job description and work assignments, what work skills are required for you to perform your overall job successfully? Please circle.

Receptionist	Shorthand	Editing	Custodial
Typing	Transcription	Layout	Machine repair
Computer operations	Grammar	Art Work	Painting
Filing	Spelling	PBX	Furniture repair
Human Relations	Punctuation	Communications	Carpentry
Other (name)	Other (name)	Other (name)	Equipment operator
			Other (name)

2. In which of the work skills you have checked, do you feel you excel?

3. In which of the work skills you have checked, do you feel you need to improve, if any?

4. What improvement plan do you propose?

5. What frustration, if any, do you encounter in performing your job?

6. In what ways, if any, could your supervisor be of greater help to you in the performance of your job?

7. On what tasks, duties, have you spent most of your time during the last six months?

8. Do you have any comments, suggestions on work improvements, or whatever, that you would like to discuss with your supervisor?

F-3

9. How would you rate your performance on the job in the following areas? Place a check in the space you feel appropriate.

	Below Satisfactory Level	Satisfactory Level	Surpasses Satisfactory Level	Far Exceeds Satisfactory Level	Effectiveness	
	0 - 4.5	5.0 - 6.5	7.0 - 8.5	9.0-10.0	ER	SR
1. Work Skills Ability	Refers to the effective application of work skills required					
2. Quantity of Work	How much acceptable is produced in a given time?					
3. Quality of Work	How thorough, accurate, and acceptable is the work performed?					
4. Work Relationships	How cooperative and how well one works as a team member					
5. Work Habits	Refers to initiative, dependability, attendance, punctuality, manner of work					
6. Innovation	Refers to new ideas, systems, and methods					
7. Self Improvement Progress	Refers to extent a person improves oneself for great work performance					
				Total Divided by 7		
				Average		

ER = Employee Rating   SR = Supervisor Rating

_____   _____
Signature of Supervisor   Date

F-4

EMPLOYEE PERFORMANCE REVIEW

(To be completed by employee)

Employee _____ Job Title _____ Date _____

1. What goals were agreed upon for the period under consideration?

_____

_____

_____

_____

2. Were you able to attain these goals? if not, which one was not attained? Why?

_____

_____

_____

3. What do you feel is the single biggest problem you face in performing your work?

(1) Over which you have control	(2) Which is outside your control

4. In what ways can your work performance be improved?

_____

_____

_____

_____

5. In what ways could your supervisor be of greater help in attaining your goals?

_____

_____

_____

6. List any areas of your job which you feel need clarification.

_____

_____

_____

PERFORMANCE REVIEW

To be completed by supervisor

Ratings

Outstanding	(+)	Satisfactory	(-)	Below Standard

Job Knowledge-Consider degree of familiarity with all phases of regular duties.
Comment

Quality of Work-Consider degree of accuracy, neatness, completeness of work.
Comment:

Quantity of Work-Consider degree of volume of satisfactory work produced under normal conditions.
Comment:

Attitude and Cooperation-Consider attitude towards job and success in cooperating and working efficiently with others.
Comment:

Personality-Consider the over-all impression made on others.
Comment:

Dependability-Consider degree of reliability in performing assigned tasks, dependability in following instructions and being on the job with minimum loss of time.
Comment:

Adaptability-Consider degree of ability to meet changing conditions and the ease with which new duties are learned.
Comment:

Leadership-Consider ability to develop subordinates, instill respect, loyalty, establish unified action, accept and delegate responsibility, maintain high morale, represent management.
Comment:

INTEREST GROUP APPRAISAL
Instruction Sheet

This is an Interest Group Appraisal of _____, who serves on our staff as _____. You have been selected to give this appraisal because of your interest or involvement in areas of our church program supervised or implemented by this staff member.

These staff appraisals are performed for the purpose of aiding our staff members in leading the church in the best possible way. Not only are our staff members in favor of having an appraisal system, but they initiated the idea and largely designed it. The leadership, secretarial, and custodial staff members hope you share their desire that our church fulfill our Lord's greatest expectations in this modern day.

You are to give an appraisal of this staff member under the fourteen categories listed on the following sheets. Under each category you will find five possible choices. These are your answers. For instance, under the category entitled "Christian Character" you are to choose the statement underneath that category which best describes the person you are appraising. Please place a ☑ in the small square in the lower-right hand corner of the answer you choose. You may also add written comments that seem appropriate. **Remember to mark only one answer under each category.** If you have not observed this person to the point that you can choose an answer, simply check the square marked "Not observed."

Please complete this appraisal as soon as possible and return it to the office in this envelope. Do not sign your name. Your appraisal will be kept completely anonymous. Thank you once again for helping us.

The Personnel Committee

INTEREST GROUP APPRAISAL

CHRISTIAN CHARACTER		COMMENTS	COOPERATION		COMMENTS
Consistently demonstrates love, patience and forgiveness toward others.	☐		Enjoys working with others. Willingly assists others without sacrificing personal efficiency.	☐	
Understands relationship between Christian character and good workmanship.	☐		Works well with others. Will assist others when needed.	☐	
Christian lifestyle is clearly observable.	☐		Not disturbed by others working nearby. Will assist when requested by supervisor.	☐	
Inconsistent as a Christian example.	☐		Easily disturbed by others working nearby. Will assist when crises exists.	☐	
Doesn't understand Christian standards.	☐		Doesn't enjoy working with others. Works effectively only when alone.	☐	
Not observed.	☐		Not observed.	☐	

INTEREST GROUP APPRAISAL

ATTITUDE	COMMENTS	RELATING TO PEOPLE	COMMENTS
Consistently cheerful and positive toward work and people. Never upset.		Elicites excellent response from all age groups.	
Normally cheerful and positive. Not easily upset.		Consistently has good rapport with people.	
Usually cheerful and positive. Sometimes moody.		Gets a good response from most people.	
Seldom cheerful and positive. Often moody.		Sometimes tactless and upsetting.	
Never cheerful and positive. Usually moody.		Usually angers people.	
Not observed.		Not observed.	

INTEREST GROUP APPRAISAL

QUANTITY OF WORK		COMMENTS	QUALITY OF WORK		COMMENTS
Produces an exceptional amount of work.	☐		Final product of work is highly accurate and in excellent form.	☐	
Produces an unusual amount of work.	☐		Final product of work is accurate and in adequate form.	☐	
Produces an acceptable amount of work.	☐		Final product of work is accurate and in acceptable form.	☐	
Produces less work than normally expected.	☐		Final product of work is fairly accurate and usually in acceptable form.	☐	
Produces an inadequate amount of work.	☐		Final product of work is often inaccurate and in unacceptable form.	☐	
Not observed.	☐		Not observed.	☐	

INTEREST GROUP APPRAISAL

RESPONSIBILITY	COMMENTS		INITIATIVE AND CREATIVITY	COMMENTS
Highly responsible worker. Looks upon job as a ministry.		☐	Resourceful; imaginative. Always looks for ways to increase efficiency.	☐
Unusually responsible worker. Is devoted to the position.		☐	Proceeds on work without prompting. Frequently offers suggestions.	☐
Takes assigned responsibility seriously. Sometimes seeks additional assignments.		☐	Proceeds on work without prompting. Occasionally makes suggestions.	☐
Somewhat responsible person. Sees responsibility as added pressure.		☐	Often needs help getting started. Seldom makes suggestions.	☐
Refuses to accept responsibility.		☐	Must be told what to do. Never makes suggestions.	☐
Not observed.			Not observed.	☐

INTEREST GROUP APPRAISAL

ORGANIZATION AND PLANNING	COMMENTS	KNOWLEDGE OF JOB	COMMENTS
Has superior skills in organizing and planning. ☐		Exceptionally knowledgeable about job. Needs no supervision. ☐	
Has unusual skills in organizing and planning. ☐		Better knowledge than normally expected. Seldom needs supervision. ☐	
Has above average skills in organizing and planning. ☐		Sufficient knowledge of job. Occasionally needs supervision. ☐	
Has fair skills in organizing and planning. ☐		Lacks adequate knowledge of job. Excessive supervision required. ☐	
Has inadequate skills in organizing and planning. ☐		Doesn't understand job. Needs constant supervision. ☐	
Not observed. ☐		Not observed. ☐	

INTEREST GROUP APPRAISAL

DEPENDABILITY	COMMENTS	TENACITY	COMMENTS
Exceptionally dependable. Never fails to deliver.		Works to completion on assigned and regular projects.	
Unusually dependable. Almost always delivers.		Seldom quits work on projects before they are complete.	
Often dependable. Will normally deliver.		Will eventually complete most projects.	
Often undependable. Seldom delivers.		Often follows through with plans.	
Cannot be depended upon. Never delivers.		Never completes planned work.	
Not observed.		Not observed.	

INTEREST GROUP APPRAISAL

PUNCTUALITY	COMMENTS	PERSONAL APPEARANCE	COMMENTS
Seldom late to work or misses deadlines.	☐	Consistently well groomed. Very neat.	☐
Occasionally late but for good reasons.	☐	Careful about appearance. Good taste in dress.	☐
Is sometimes late without acceptable reason.	☐	Generally neat and attractive.	☐
Frequently late to work and with assignments.	☐	Sometimes untidy and ill kept.	☐
Consistently late to work and with assignments.	☐	Always untidy. Poor taste in dress.	☐
Not observed.		Not observed.	

TO: ALL SUPERVISORY STAFF

FROM:

SUBJECT: Personnel Evaluations

DATE:

Attached you will find copies of the personnel evaluation that you are responsible for completing. The form contains twenty character and ability traits with a definition of each. Right above the first character trait (Accuracy) is a rating scale that is equal to the following numerical equivalents:

Definitely Unsatisfactory		Below Expected		Satisfactory		Above Expected		Outstanding	
-	+	-	+	-	+	-	+	-	+
.5	1	1.5	2	2.5	3	3.5	4	4.5	5

Please put the corresponding numerical equivalent on the rating scale blank line that best exemplifies the person for that trait.

Example:

Accuracy . . .

		2.5		

One of the traits requires your knowledge of the persons "Standards of Performance." These should already have been listed and should accompany their job descriptions. If these standards of performance do not exist, please secure a copy of the form and have them prepared and returned to administration along with the completed evaluation form.

The fourth page is provided for the supervisor to counsel with the employee. After you have completed the form, add the twenty numerical ratings and divide by 20 for the average rating. Note it on the bottom of the fourth page in the circle. Have the employee sign the evaluation and provide them a copy. Return the original to administration by _____.

If you have any questions concerning this form, please contact me.

Performance Appraisal

. . . .

Employee Name _____ Job Title _____ Hire Date _____

Length of time you have managed employee's performance_____

Appraisal Period From _____ To _____ Appraiser _____ Date _____

. . . .

Instructions:

A.   Complete the background data at the top of this page.

B.   Listed below are a number of traits, abilities and characteristics that are important for the success of our ministry. Place a numerical score over the descriptive phrase which most nearly describes the person being rated.

C.   Two common mistakes in rating are: 1) Appraiser tendency to rate nearly everyone as "average" on every trait instead of being more critical in judgment. The appraiser should use the ends of the scale as well as the middle; 2) The "halo effect," i.e., a tendency to rate the same individual "excellent" on every trait or "poor" on every trait based on the overall picture one has of the person being rated. However, each person has strong points and weak points and these should be indicated according to the rating scale just below:

Definitely Unsatisfactory		Below Expected		Satisfactory		Above Expected		Outstanding	
-	+	-	+	-	+	-	+	-	+
.5	1	1.5	2	2.5	3	3.5	4	4.5	5

1.   ACCURACY is the correctness of work duties performed.

Accuracy of work is unsatisfactory	Careless; makes recurrent errors. Substandard accuracy	Usually accurate; makes only average number of mistakes	Requires little supervision; is exact and precise most of time.	Requires absolute minimum of supervision; is most always accurate.

2.   ALERTNESS is the ability to grasp instructions, to meet changing conditions and to solve novel or problem situations

Slow to grasp instructions & learn new jobs.	Requires more than average instructions and explanations.	Grasps instructions with average ability.	Usually quick to understand instructions & learn new jobs.	Exceptionally able to learn new jobs and adapt to new situations.

3.   ATTAINMENT against standards of performance.

Definitely Unsatisfactory.	Substandard but making progress.	Doing an average job.	Definitely above average.	Outstanding.

Definitely Unsatisfactory		Below Expected		Satisfactory		Above Expected		Outstanding	
-	+	-	+	-	+	-	+	-	+
.5	1	1.5	2	2.5	3	3.5	4	4.5	5

4. ATTENDANCE is faithfulness in coming to work daily and conforming to work hours.

Often absent without sufficient reason and.or frequently reports for work late.	Below standards in attendance and/or reporting for work on time.	Present and on time as expected.	Very prompt; regular in attendance.	Always regular and prompt; available for overtime when needed.

5. ATTITUDE is the feelings or emotions displayed toward the job and fellow employees.

Unsatisfactory attitude for the job.	Frequently displays a poor attitude	Generally acceptable attitude.	Very good attitude; nice to be around.	Excellent attitude.

6. CONFIDENTIALITY is the ability to be entrusted with confidences.

Gossiper, quick to reveal confidences.	Needs reminding to hold confidences.	Fairly reliable with confidences.	Can be trusted with most confidences.	Holds statements in the strictest confidences.

7. COOPERATION is the ability to work with others.

Uncooperative hard to work with.	Sometimes resents helping out or being helped.	Usually willing to help or receive help.	Always available & willing to help or be helped.	Excellent cooperation with others.

8. COURTESY is the polite attention an individual gives other people.

Blunt; discourteous antagonistic.	Sometimes discourteous.	Agreeable and pleasant.	Always very polite and pleasant.	Inspiring to others in being courteous and very pleasant.

9. CREATIVITY is the talent for having new ideas, for finding new and better ways of doing things and for being imaginative.

Rarely has a new idea; is unimaginative.	Occasionally comes up with a new idea.	Has average imagination; has reasonable number of new ideas.	Frequently suggests better ways of doing things; is very imaginative.	Continually seeks new and better ways of doing things; is extremely imaginative.

10. DEDICATION is the degree of devotion one has for the job or ministry.

Very little dedication.	Sometimes questionable.	Satisfactory, no cause for questioning.	Sets a high example to follow.	Total devotion to the task.

Definitely Unsatisfactory		Below Expected		Satisfactory		Above Expected		Outstanding	
-	+	-	+	-	+	-	+	-	+
.5	1	1.5	2	2.5	3	3.5	4	4.5	5

11. DEPENDABILITY is the ability to do required jobs well with a minimum of supervision

Requires close supervision; is unreliable.	Sometimes requires prompting.	Usually takes care of necessary tasks and completes with reasonable promptness.	Requires little supervision; is reliable.	Requires absolute minimum of supervision.

12. DRIVE is the desire to attain goals, to achieve.

Has poorly defined goals and acts without purpose; puts forth practically no effort.	Sets goals too low; puts forth little effort to achieve.	Has average goals and usually puts forth effort to reach these.	Strives hard; has high desire to achieve.	Sets high goals and strives to reach these.

13. FRIENDLINESS is the sociability and warmth which an individual imparts in one's attitude toward customers, other employees; supervisor, and the persons one may supervise.

Very distant and aloof. Generally not friendly.	At times not friendly.	Warm; friendly; sociable.	Very sociable and friendly.	Extremely friendly; excellent at estab lishing good will.

14. HOUSEKEEPING is the orderliness and cleanliness in which an individual keeps his work area.

Disorderly or untidy.	Some tendency to be careless and untidy.	Ordinarily keeps work area fairly neat.	Quite conscientious about neatness and cleanliness.	Unusually neat, clean and orderly.

15. JOB KNOWLEDGE is the information concerning work duties which an individual should know for a satisfactory job performance.

Poorly informed about work duties	Lacks knowledge of some phases of work.	Moderately inform- ed; can answer most job related questions.	Understands all phases of work.	Has complete mastery of all phases of job.

16. PERSONALITY is an individual's behavior characteristics or his personal suitability for the job.

Personality unsatis- factory for this job	Personality may not be suited for this job.	Personality satisfactory for this job.	Very desirable personality for this job.	Outstanding personality for this job.

Definitely Unsatisfactory		Below Expected		Satisfactory		Above Expected		Outstanding	
-	+	-	+	-	+	-	+	-	+
.5	1	1.5	2	2.5	3	3.5	4	4.5	5

17. PERSONAL APPEARANCE is the personal impression an individual makes on others. (Consider cleanliness, grooming, neatness and appropriateness of dress on the job.)

Very untidy; poor taste in dress.	Sometimes untidy and careless about personal appearance.	Generally neat and clean; satisfactory personal appearance.	Careful about personal appearance; good taste in dress.	Unusually well groomed; very neat; excellent taste in dress.

18. PHYSICAL FITNESS is the ability to work consistently and with only moderate fatigue. (Consider physical alertness and energy.)

Tires easily; may not be physically able to perform job.	Frequently tires and is slow.	Meets physical and energy job requirements.	Energetic; seldom tires.	Excellent health; alert and energetic.

19. QUANTITY OF WORK is the amount of work an individual does in a work day.

Does not meet minimum quantity requirements.	Quantity of work below expected level.	Volume of work is satisfactory.	Very industrious; does more than is required.	Superior work production record.

20. STABILITY is the ability to withstand pressure and to remain calm in crisis situations.

Conduct becomes unsatisfactory under pressure; is nervous and unstable.	Occasionally unstable under pressure; is easily irritated.	Has average tolerance for crisis; usually remains calm.	Tolerates most pressure; likes crises more than the average person.	Performs well under pressure; really effective at solving crisis situations.

COMMENTS

Major weak points are --

1. _____
2. _____
3. _____

and these can be strengthened by doing the following:

_____
_____
_____
_____
_____
_____
_____
_____
_____

Major strong points are --

1. _____
2. _____
3. _____

and these can be used more effectively by doing the following:

_____
_____
_____
_____
_____
_____
_____
_____
_____

Rated by _____   _____
                     (Name)   (Title)

A copy of this report has been given to me and has been discussed with me.

_____ _____
(Employee's Signature)   (Date)

_____

Rating

EMPLOYEE'S PERSONAL EVALUATION

Employee's Name _____

Date:_____

Employee's
Self Evaluation of Performance

Strengths: _____

_____

_____

_____

_____

_____

Weaknesses:_____

_____

_____

_____

_____

_____

Opportunities: _____

_____

_____

_____

_____

Threats: _____

_____

_____

_____

_____

_____

Strategies _____

_____

_____

_____

_____

MERIT RATING REPORT

This rating form is intended to indicate job performance. Read all phrases in each series, then circle the one which seems to fit the employee best. Use your own independent judgment. Add comments on the other side if needed.

EMPLOYEE _____ Date _____

Quality of work: exceptional   superior   good   acceptable   inferior

Quantity of work: more than adequate   adequate   less than adequate

Personal Appearance: always acceptable   generally acceptable   offensive

Loyalty to the Church: high   acceptable   low nonexistent

Attitude toward the job: eager   willing   interest wavers   indifferent

Attitude toward other workers: highly cooperative   usually cooperative   indifferent troublesome

Attitude toward supervisor: highly cooperative   usually cooperative   indifferent
reluctant   resentful

Attitude toward improvement: improves voluntarily   improves with suggestion
shows no improvementt   reacts negatively

Promptness in dispatching work: consistently on time   requires reminding
often late   always late

Accuracy: rare errors   occasional errors   frequent errors

Initiative: exceptional   good   acceptable   nonexistent

Tidiness: consistent   spasmodic   nonexistent

Attendance record: perfect   occasionally late or absent   chronically bad, with cause
chronically bad, without cause

All things considered this employee is: outstanding   good   acceptable   poor

This employ is eligible for a merit increase on:

_____ to $_____

Do you recommend this merit increase? _____

Signed _____

NACBA - Performance Evaluation

Name of Employee _____

Title/Position _____

   Instructions. The following five statements describe the characteristics of worker. Indicate your agreement or disagreement with each statement by carefully checking the blank that best describes your feelings.

a. **Worker carries out task assignments efficiently.**

Strongly agree	_____
Moderately agree	_____
Tend to agree	_____
Tend to disagree	_____
Moderately disagree	_____
Strongly disagree	_____

b. **Worker adapts readily to changes in task requirements.**

Strongly agree	_____
Moderately agree	_____
Tend to agree	_____
Tend to disagree	_____
Moderately disagree	_____
Strongly disagree	_____

c. **Worker is involved in interpersonal conflicts that interfere with work progress.**

Strongly agree	_____
Moderately agree	_____
Tend to agree	_____
Tend to disagree	_____
Moderately disagree	_____
Strongly disagree	_____

d. **Worker expresses job satisfaction.**

Strongly agree	_____
Moderately agree	_____
Tend to agree	_____
Tend to disagree	_____
Moderately disagree	_____
Strongly disagree	_____

e. **Worker achieves task goals successfully.**

Strongly agree	_____
Moderately agree	_____
Tend to agree	_____
Tend to disagree	_____
Moderately disagree	_____
Strongly disagree	_____

Supervisor _____

Signature _____ Date _____

NACBA - Performance Evaluation

Employee's Name _____

Job Title_____

How long has employee been under your supervision? _____

	Outstanding	Above Average	Average	Below Average.	Unsatis-factory	Not Related to Job Success	Unable to Rate
1. Productivity							
2. Job Knowledge							
3. Judgment							
4. Initiative							
5. Cooperativeness							
6. Teamwork							

SUPERVISOR'S COMMENTS:

Overall Rating:

Additional Comments:

Date Rated _____

Date Discussed _____

_____
Supervisor's Signature

1. **Productivity:** The actual work output of the staff member relative to other staff based on actual production rather than productive capability.

2. **Job Knowledge:** Knowledge of the techniques, skills, processes, procedures, products, equipment and materials required to do this job properly.

3. **Judgment:** The extent to which the staff member makes sound decisions. Freedom from impulsiveness and immaturity in his/her thinking. Ability to base actions on fact rather than emotion.

4. **Initiative:** The degree to which staff member acts independently in new situations; the extent to which he/she sees what needs to be done and does it without being told.

5. **Cooperativeness:** Willingness to work harmoniously with others in getting a job done. Readiness to observe and conform to the policies of management. Keeping an attitude toward others that makes working together comfortable.

6. **Teamwork:** Effectiveness in planning, organizing, and communicating the work with team members and in winning their cooperation. General effectiveness in getting work done through a high trust level with team members.

PERFORMANCE REVIEW (APPRAISAL)

Purpose: The purpose of the performance appraisal is to provide useful and helpful information for both the church and its employees.

For the individual employee the performance appraisal provides the basis for sound coaching and counseling on how and where to improve performance. It also provides satisfaction and enables the employee to know precisely what the job is and some special ways performance can be improved.

For the church, the performance appraisal provides a way to evaluate how effectively the paid staff are meeting the mission of the church through the fulfilling of their job descriptions. It provides a way to adjust performance to meet the requirements of their position or the needs of the congregation. It provides a means of identifying those employees who have the potential to carry broader responsibilities and contribute further to the growth of the church. It also provides a means of assessing salary increases and other rewards and benefits.

Frequency: The first appraisal will be made after the first three months of employment.

The second appraisal will be scheduled after six months of employment.

After the first six months of employment, appraisals will be scheduled every six months through the first two years of employment.

After two years of employment, appraisals will be scheduled annually.

If at any time conditions warrant it, the appraisal may be scheduled sooner than indicated above. Conditions may be either excellent or poor performance.

Instrument: The performance appraisal form will consist of a supervisor review and a consultative review.

The supervisor review will be based on observations about personal characteristics and skills and the meeting of requirements of the job description.

The consultative review will be based on mutually agreed upon key objectives and competency development.

A weight will be given for each portion of the appraisal based on the length of employment. The weight or value given each section will be as follows:

Year	Supervisor	Consultative
First	100%	0%
Second	80%	20%
Third	50%	50%
Fourth and following	30%	70%

Process: At the scheduled time of appraisal the consultative team will meet with the employee to review the appraisal.

The consultative team, selected by the Staff/Parish Relations Committee, will consist of the following persons:

      a. the supervisor

      b. a respected member of the church (may be a member of the staff parish committee.)

      c. someone familiar with the area in which the employee works.

The consultative team participates in the supervisor review as well as the consultative review.

The supervisor review will be a straight forward evaluation of the employees fulfillment of job expectations.

The consultative review will consist of the following elements.

1. The team will assist the employee to develop a list of 2 to 4 key objectives that the employee would like to accomplish during the coming year. These objectives have to do with the development of areas of the job description. The objectives may define specific results the employee wants to accomplish, new ideas for doing the job, or plans of how things can be done differently. The employee will be responsible for bringing a list of suggested objectives to the meeting from which the 2 to 4 key objectives will be developed. The purpose here is to let the employee use his or her ability to improve their job.

2. The employee also develops a list of 1 or 2 specific competencies in which they would like to improve. These would be specific skills that add to the effectiveness of their job performance.

3. The first list of key objectives and specific competencies will be developed at the first year appraisal time.

4. These objectives and competency goals are listed on the performance appraisal form.

5. Each succeeding appraisal event will consist of evaluating the previous key objectives and specific competencies and developing new ones.

The employee will have the right to write comments on the appraisal form that reflects any agreement or disagreement with the evaluation of the supervisor.

Mutual agreement is sought for the consultative appraisal among the consultative team with the employee.

Results: The performance appraisal, signed by all participants, becomes a part of the employees personnel file.

Copies are given to the employee.

Results are shared with the Staff Parish Committee for review as to the mission of the church and consideration of benefits and rewards.

PERFORMANCE APPRAISAL

NAME: _____ POSITION: _____

Date of employment: Report by (Supervisor)   Date of Report:

<u>**SUPERVISOR APPRAISAL**</u>

1. - Not satisfactory   2. - Satisfactory   3. - Good   4. - Excellent   N/O/A/ - Not Observed or Not Applicable

A space is provided at the end of each category so that the supervisor can give a brief statement when either column 1 or column 4 is checked.

		NOA	1	2	3	4
ATTITUDE Consider employee's general attitude on the job and around other employees and church members/friends	A. Toward job - Enthusiasm and interest					
	B. Toward church members/friends - Courtesy, helpful and appearance					
	C. Toward other employees - Ability to work with others					
	D. Toward church - Loyalty and cooperation					
QUALITY AND QUANTITY OF WORK	A. Knowledge of job - Ability to get job done					
	B. Performance - Ability to get job done right and dependably					
	C. Timeliness - Being on time, completing jobs on time					
ABILITY TO PLAN AND ORGANIZE Consider performance and results achieved	A. Plans work well					
	B. Follows through on plans					
	C. Communicates well with other employees and volunteers					
	D. Meets emergency situations promptly					
INITIATIVE Consider ability to think independently and constructively	A. Self starter					
	B. Develops constructive ideas					
	C. Contributes practical suggestions					

		NOA	1	2	3	4
JUDGEMENT AND DECISION Consider ability to handle emergency as well as routine decisions	A. Exercises good judgement					
	B. Makes prompt and accurate decisions					
	C. Assumes full responsibility					
EXECUTION OF CHURCH POLICIES Consider ability to gain adherence to church policy	A. Understands policies and reasons thereof					
	B. Applies knowledge of policies to decisions					
	C. Instills desire in others to follow church policy					
CHURCH MEMBER/FRIEND RELATIONS	A. Treats members/friends with courtesy and respect					
	B. Performs duties in a manner that satisfies members/friends expectations and needs					
CARE AND SAFETY OF EQUIPMENT	A. Care of church equipment - using, cleaning, storing					
	B. Safety in operating church equipment					

THIS SECTION IS FOR THOSE WITH SUPERVISORY RESPONSIBILITIES

		NOA	1	2	3	4
ABILITY TO DIRECT AND DEVELOP EMPLOYEES/ VOLUNTEERS Consider leadership qualities	A. Motivates employees/volunteers to accomplish objectives					
	B. Delegates authority					
	C. Instills enthusiasm					
	D. Obtains prompt and full cooperation					

SUMMARY: This space is provided so that you may add any additional remarks about the individual being appraised. It may also be used by the employee to respond to any evaluations or comments

AVERAGE SCORE THIS SECTION _____ WEIGHT _____

CONSULTATIVE APPRAISAL

KEY OBJECTIVES: Rate your progress on your Key Objectives for the current year.

1.					
2.					
3.					

	NOA	1	2	3	4
4.					
COMPETENCY DEVELOPMENT GOALS: Rate your progress on your Competency Development for the current year.					
1.					
2.					

STRENGTHS:

WEAKNESSES:

_____

AVERAGE SCORE THIS SECTION _____ WEIGHT _____

TOTAL SCORE _____

Signature of employee: _____ Date _____
Signature of supervisor: _____ Date _____
Signature of consultant: _____ Date _____
Signature of consultant: _____ Date _____

CONSULTATIVE GOALS FOR THE COMING YEAR

KEY OBJECTIVES: List your Key Objectives for the coming year.

1.

2.

3.

4.

COMPETENCY DEVELOPMENT: List your Competency Development goals for the coming year.

1.

2.

PERFORMANCE AND SALARY REVIEW RECOMMENDATION

Employee _____ Job Title _____

Supervisor _____ Date _____

Satisfactory Performance Level

	FAR EXCEEDS	SURPASSES	SATISFACTORY	BEGINNING BELOW
QUALITY OF WORK (How well is work performed?)				
QUANTITY OF WORK (Amount of acceptable work)				
WORK RELATIONSHIPS (Effectiveness as a Team Member)				
WORK HABITS (Dependable, punctual)				
SELF-STARTER (Alert-Active-Creative)				
SELF-IMPROVEMENT (Performance improves through job related activities and training)				

Present Pay Grade _____ Step _____

Date of last salary increase _____

Present salary $ _____

☐ Recommended Increase $ _____

☐ Increase Not Recommended - Next Review Date Set_____

Salary after increase $ _____

Approval Date _____ Effective Date _____

Signature of Supervisor _____

M-1

EMPLOYEE EVALUATION CHECK LIST

A check list of items which can be used effectively to "grade" employees as a part of your annual employee evaluation process.

	Employee Name
	Supervisor Name
	Scale 1 of 10 (10 highest grade)

1. Self starter; takes initiative _____

2. Perceives and follows instructions _____

3. Works independently _____

4. Compatibility to clients and co-workers _____

5. Mature judgments _____

6. Willingness to apply self to tasks _____

7. Desire for excellence _____

8. Professional in appearance, style and attitude _____

9. Technical competency _____

10. Thoroughness/follow through _____

11. Integrity with self and others _____

12. Interest in learning and improvement of self _____

13. Client interest versus self interest _____

14. Loyalty to employer _____

15. Willingness to accept criticism _____

16. Spiritual compatibility, etc. _____

17. Degree of satisfaction with salary and benefits _____

18. Degree of communication/understands the boss _____

19. Degree of "I have done a good job at my work here." _____

20. Degree of job satisfaction/fulfillment _____

Total _____

PERFORMANCE GUIDE FOR EVALUATING EMPLOYEES

DEGREES → FACTORS	FAR EXCEEDS JOB REQUIREMENTS	EXCEEDS JOB REQUIREMENTS	MEETS JOB REQUIREMENTS	NEEDS SOME IMPROVEMENTS	DOES NOT MEET MINIMUM REQUIREMENTS
Quality	Leaps tall buildings with a single bound.	Must take running start to leap over tall buildings.	Can leap over short buildings only.	Crashes into buildings when attempting to jump over them.	Cannot recognize building at a glance.
Timeliness	Is faster than a speeding bullet.	Is as fast as a speeding bullet.	Not quite as fast as a speeding bullet.	Would you believe a slow bullet.	Wounds self with bullets when attempting to shoot.
Initiative	Is stronger than a locomotive.	Is stronger than a bull elephant.	Is stronger than a bull.	Shoots the bull.	Believes cock and bull stories.
Adaptability	Walks on water consistently.	Walks on water in emergencies.	Washes with water.	Drinks water	Sleeps on a water bed.
Communication	Talks with God.	Talks with the angels.	Talks to himself.	Argues with himself.	Loses those arguments.

BIBLIOGRAPHY

Baird, Lloyd S., Richard W. Beatty, and Craig Eric Schneier (eds), *The Performance Appraisal Sourcebook*, Human Resource Development Press, Amherst, MA, 1982.

Berk, Ronald A. (ed), *Performance Assessment—Methods & Applications*, The Johns Hopkins University Press, Baltimore, 1986.

Block, Judy R., *Performance Appraisal on the Job: Making it Work*, Executive Enterprises Publications Co., Inc., New York, 1981.

Bloss, Julie E., *The Church Guide to Employment Law*, Church Law and Tax Report, Matthews, NC, 1993.

"Immigration Law," *Church Management: The Clergy Journal*, January 1992.

Bolt, William T., "Are Your Job Descriptions Outdated," *Church Management: The Clergy Journal*, February 1979.

Brown, Jerry W., *Church Staff Teams That Win*, Convention Press, Nashville, 1979.

Buzzard, Lynn Robert, Esq. and Susan Edwards, *Risky Business: Church Hiring and Volunteer Selection: A Legal and Policy Guide*, J.W. Edwards, Inc., Ann Arbor.

Cadwell, Charles M., *New Employee Orientation, A Practical Guide for Supervisors*, Crisp Publications, Inc., Los Altos, CA, 1988.

Callahan, Kennon L., *Twelve Keys to an Effective Church*, Harper & Row, San Francisco, 1983.

Twelve Keys to an Effective Church, The Leader's Guide, Harper & Row, San Francisco, 1987.

Chapman, Elwood N., *Attitude: Your Most Priceless Possession*, Crisp Publications, Inc., Los Altos, CA, 1990.

Your First Thirty Days: Building A Professional Image In A New Job, Crisp Publications, Inc., Menlo Park, CA, 1990.

Cook, Bruce E., *Team Building*, Distributed by Walk Thru the Bible Ministries, Inc., Atlanta, 1986.

Dale, Robert D., "Working with People," *Church Administration*, Bruce P. Powers, editor, Broadman, Nashville, 1981.

Drake Beam Morin, Inc., *Performance Management Workbook*, DBM Publishing, New York, 1993.

Eichel, Evelyn and Henry E. Bender, *Performance Appraisal: A Study of Current Techniques*, American Management Association, New York, 1984.

Engstrom, Ted W. and Edward R. Dayton, *The Art of Management for Christian Leaders*, Zondervan Publishing House, Grand Rapids, 1989.

Gorman, Ph.D., Carol Kinsey, *Managing for Commitment: Building Loyalty Within Organizations*, Crisp Publications, Inc., Menlo Park, CA, 1991.

Greenleaf, Robert K., *Servant Leadership, A Journey into The Nature of Legitimate Power and Greatness*, Paulist Press, New York, 1977.

Guidelines for Developing Church Job Descriptions, Division of Diaconal Ministry, Board of Higher Education and Ministry, The United Methodist Church, Nashville, 1988.

Hendrix, Olan, *Management for the Christian Leader*, Mott Media, Milford, MI, 1981.

Hershey, Paul and Ken Blanchard, *Management of Organizational Behavior*, Prentice-Hall, Inc., Englewood Cliffs, NJ, 1982.

Hind, James F., *The Heart and Soul of Effective Management*, Victor Books, Wheaton, IL, 1989.

Holck, Manfred, Jr., "Who is an Employee?", *Church Management: The Clergy Journal*, February 1984.

Holcomb, Tim (Comp), *Personnel Administration Guide for Southern Baptist Churches*, Convention Press, Nashville, 1988.

Hoskins, Lucy R., "Why Have a Job Description?", *Church Administration*, February 1977.

Iacocca, Lee, *Iacocca: An Autobiography*, Bantam Books, New York, 1984.

King, Patricia, *Performance Planning And Appraisal: A How-To Book For Managers*, McGraw Hill Publishers, New York, 1994.

Latham, Gary P. and Kenneth N. Wexley, *Increasing Productivity Through Performance Appraisal*, Addison-Wesley, Reading, MA, 1981.

Lewis, Alvin, "How About A Job Description?", *Church Management: The Clergy Journal*, May/June 1980.

Maddux, Robert B., *Effective Performance Appraisals*, (Revised Edition), Crisp Publications, Inc., Menlo Park, CA, 1987.

Quality Interviewing: A Step-by-Step Guide for Success, (Revised Edition), Crisp Publications, Inc., Menlo Park, CA, 1992.

Team Building: An Exercise in Leadership, A Fifty-Minute Series Book, Crisp Publications, Inc., Menlo Park, CA, 1987.

Mall, E. Jane, "Member or Not?", *Church Management: The Clergy Journal*, July 1982.

Peters, Thomas J. and Robert H. Waterman, Jr., *In Search of Excellence: Lessons From America's Best Run Companies*, Warner Books, New York, 1982.

Parchman, Joyce, (comp), *The NACBA National Church Staff Compensation Survey*, NACBA, Richardson, TX, 1995.

(comp), *Salary Administration: Why and How to Develop a Church Compensation Plan*, NACBA, Richardson, TX, 1996.

Powers, Bruce P. (ed), *Church Administration Handbook*, Abingdon, Nashville, 1985.

Rueter, Alvin C., *Personnel Management in the Church: Establishing and Implementing Personnel Policies*, Augsburg Publishing House, Minneapolis, 1984.

Rush, Myron, *Management: A Biblical Approach*, Victor Books, Wheaton, IL, 1983.

Schnake, M.E., "Apples and Oranges: Salary Review and Performance Review," *Supervisory Management*, November 1980.

Scott, Ph.D., Cynthia D. and Dennis T. Jaffee, Ph.D., *Managing Organizational Change: A Practical Guide for Managers*, Crisp Publications, Inc., Menlo Park, CA, 1989.

Shaper, Albert, *Managing Professional People: Understanding Creative Performance*, Free Press, Collie MacMillan Publishers, New York, 1985.

Steinback, Bob, *The Audit Learner: Strategies for Success*, Crisp Publications, Inc., Menlo Park, CA, 1993.

Sweeting, George, *Secrets of Excellence*, Moody Press, Chicago, 1985.

Tidwell, Charles, A., *Church Administration Effective Leadership for Ministry*, Broadman Press, Nashville, 1985.

Van Auken, Philip M., *The Well-Managed Ministry: Discovering and Developing the Strengths of Your Team*, Victor Books, Wheaton, IL, 1989.

Welch, Robert H., *The Church Organization Manual: Policies and Procedures for the Loca Church*, NACBA, Richardson, TX, 1996.